MW00988256

ISBN 978-1-4950-7721-0

7777 W. BLUEMOUND RD. P.O. BOX 13819 MILWAUKEE, WI 53213

E-Z Play® Today Music Notation © 1975 by HAL LEONARD LLC
E-Z PLAY and EASY ELECTRONIC KEYBOARD MUSIC are registered trademarks of HAL LEONARD LLC.

Visit Hal Leonard Online at
www.halleonard.com

All Out of Love

Registration 2
Rhythm: Rock or 8-Beat

Words and Music by Graham Russell
and Clive Davis

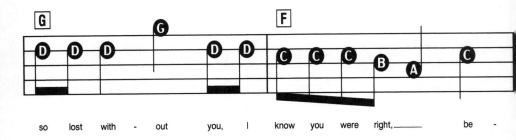

so lost with - out you, I know you were right,_____ be -

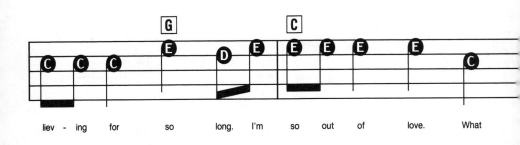

liev - ing for so long. I'm so out of love. What

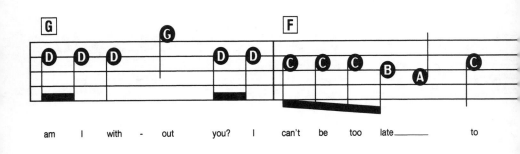

am I with - out you? I can't be too late_____ to

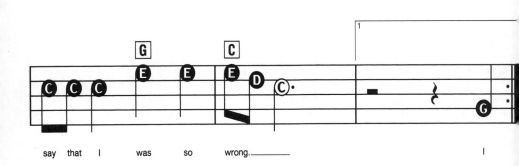

say that I was so wrong._____

2

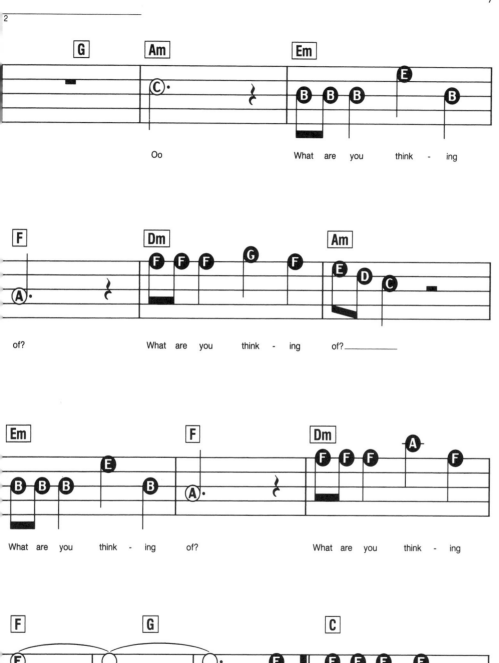

G **Am** **Em**

Oo   What are you think - ing

F **Dm** **Am**

of?   What are you think - ing of?_____

Em **F** **Dm**

What are you think - ing of?   What are you think - ing

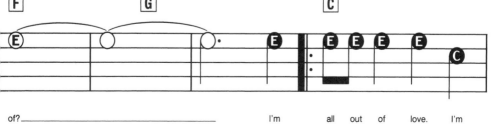

F **G** **C**

of?_____   I'm all out of love. I'm

8

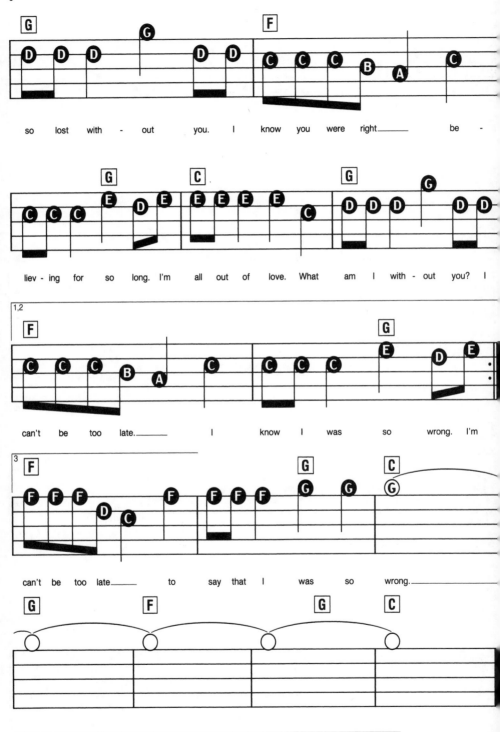

Baby, I Love Your Way

Registration 8
Rhythm: Rock or 4/4 Ballad

Words and Music by
Peter Frampton

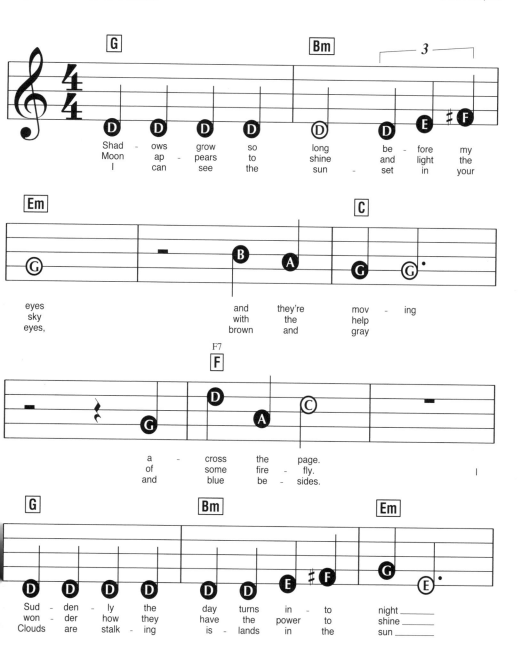

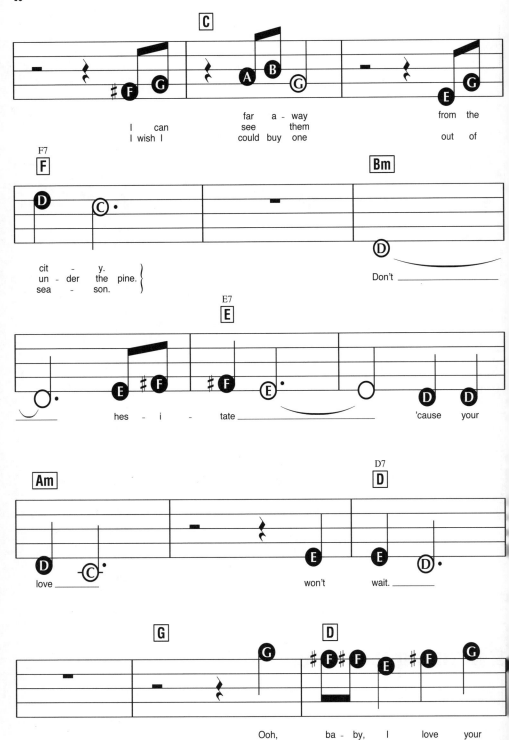

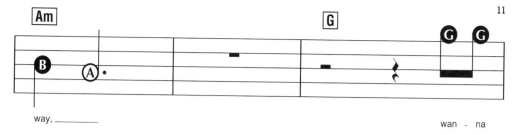

way, _____ wan - na

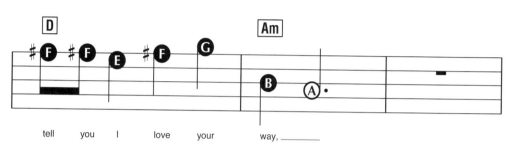

tell you I love your way, _____

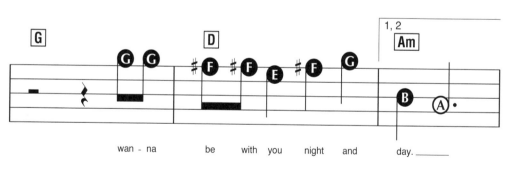

wan - na be with you night and day. _____

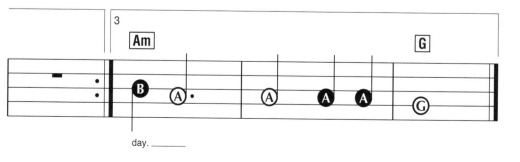

day. _____

Always on My Mind

Registration 4
Rhythm: Ballad or Slow Rock

Words and Music by Wayne Thompson,
Mark James and Johnny Christopher

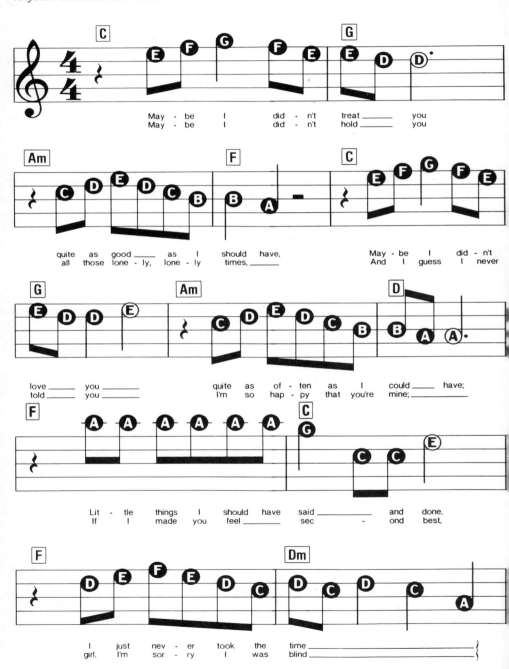

13

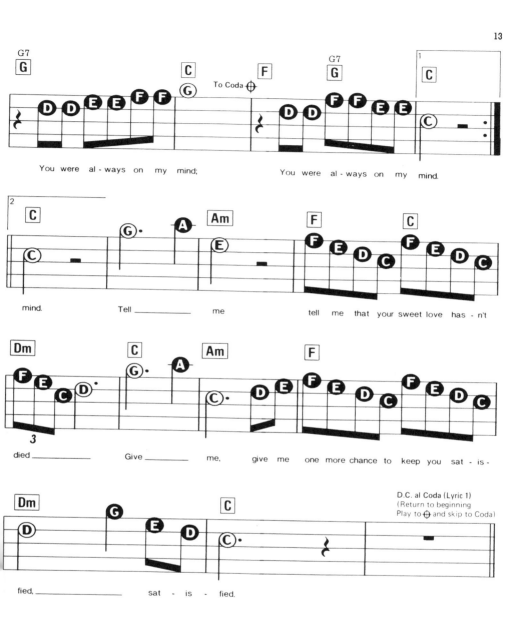

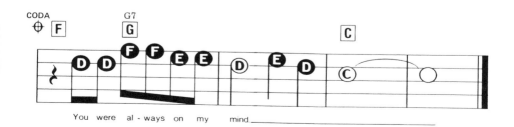

Best of My Love

Registration 8
Rhythm: Rock or Disco

Words and Music by John David Souther,
Don Henley and Glenn Frey

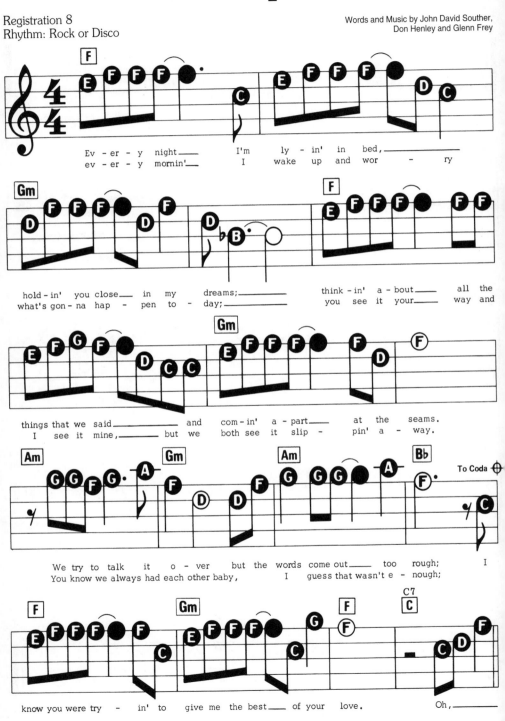

15

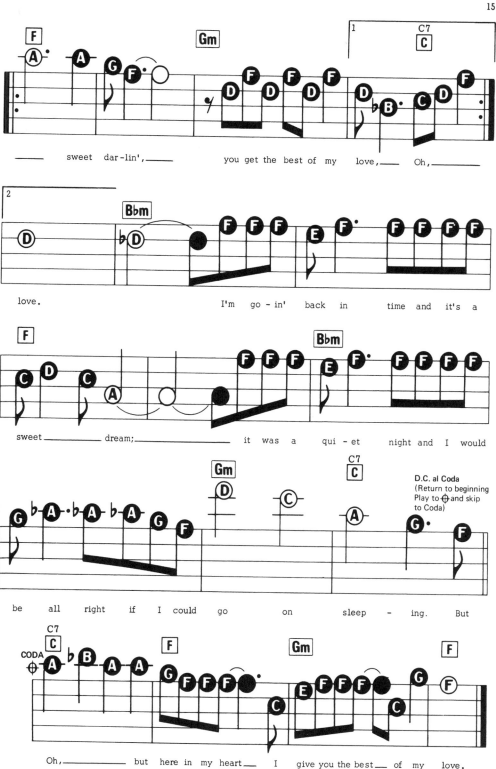

Beyond the Sea

Registration 7
Rhythm: Slow Ballad or Rock

Lyrics by Jack Lawrence
Music by Charles Trenet and Albert Lasry
Original French Lyric to "La Mer" by Charles Trenet

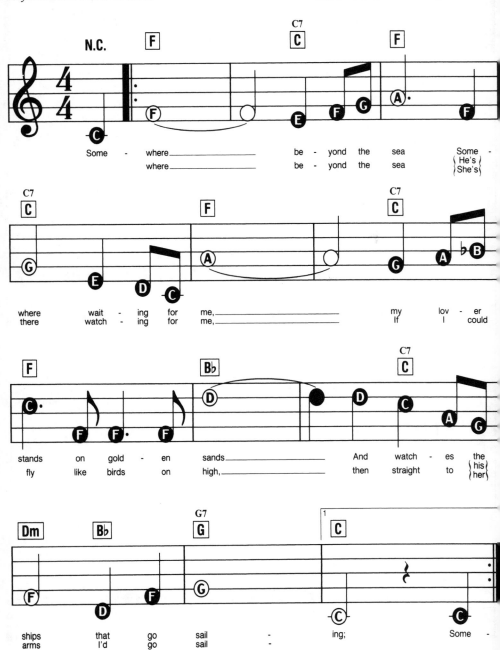

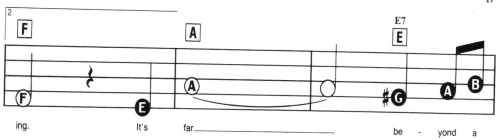

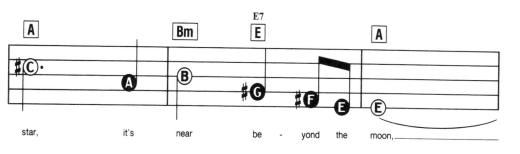

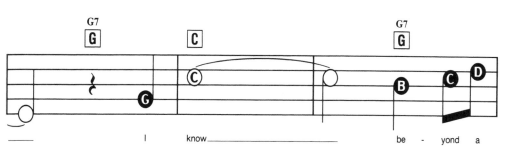

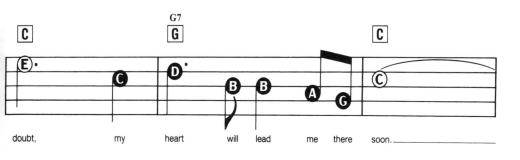

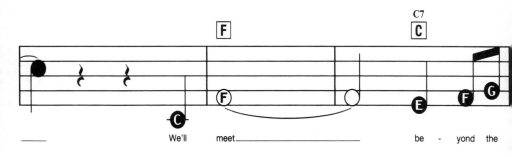

We'll meet_____ be - yond the

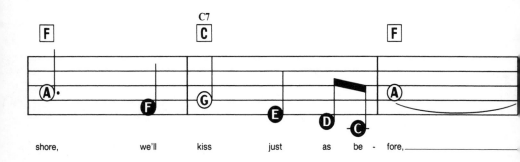

shore, we'll kiss just as be - fore,_____

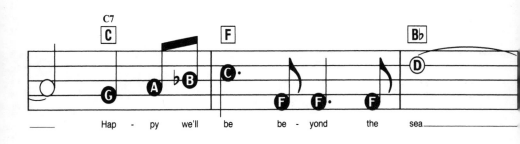

Hap - py we'll be be - yond the sea_____

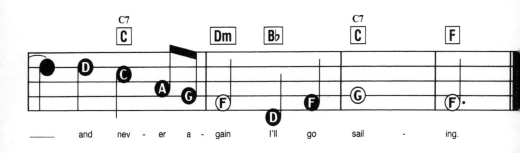

_____ and nev - er a - gain I'll go sail - ing.

Can't Smile Without You

Registration 3
Rhythm: Swing

Words and Music by Chris Arnold,
David Martin and Geoff Morrow

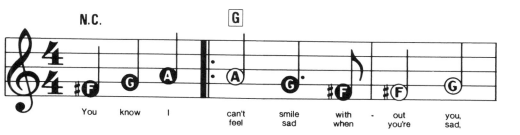

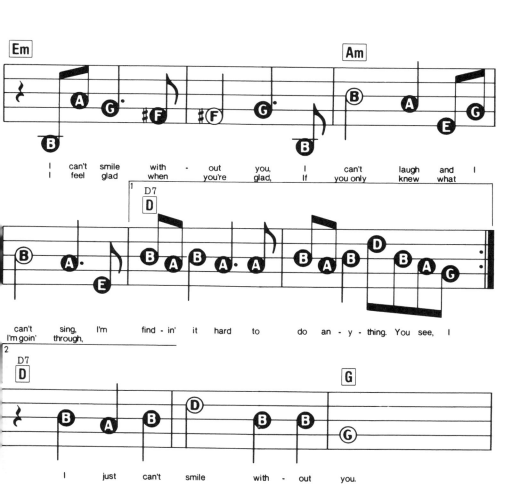

20

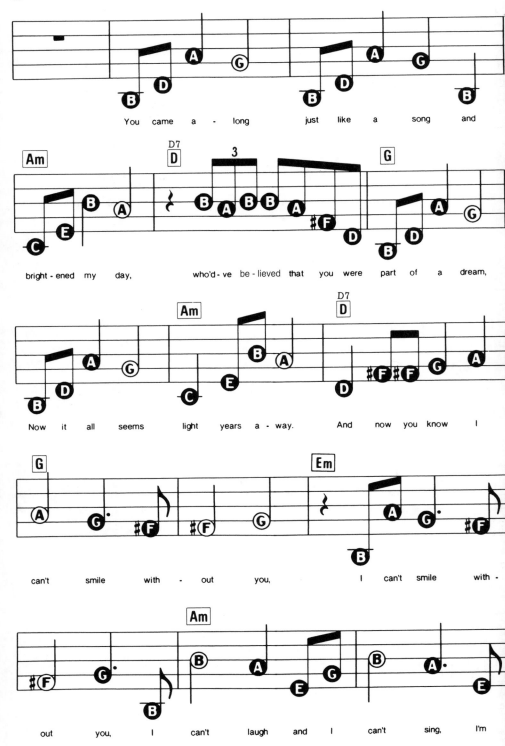

22

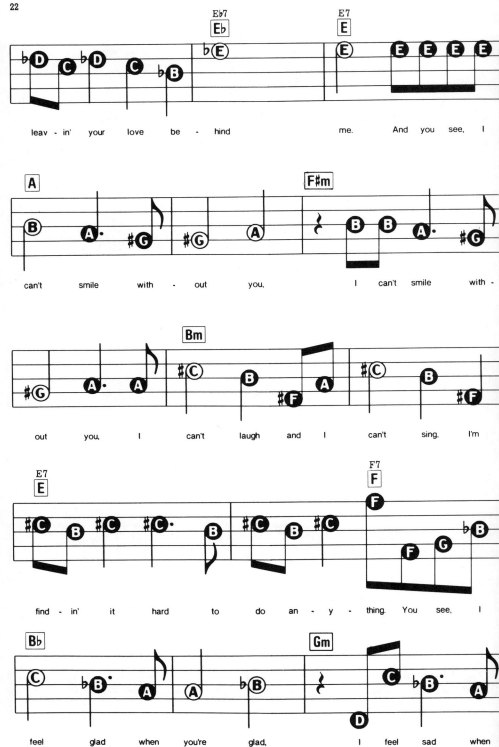

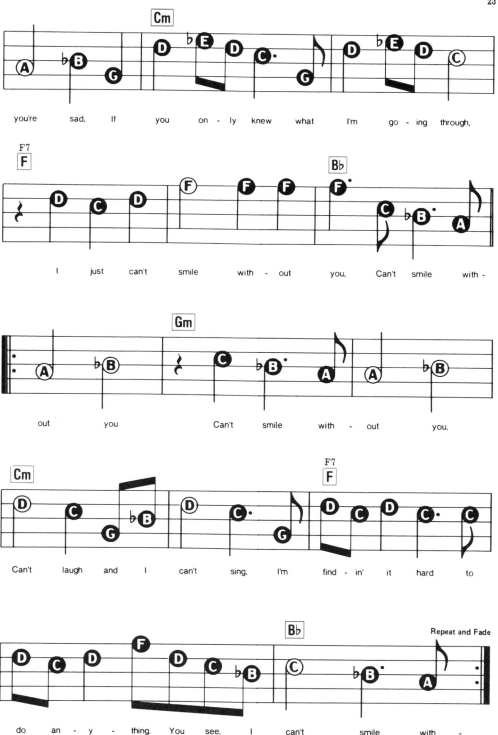

you're sad, If you on - ly knew what I'm go - ing through,

I just can't smile with - out you, Can't smile with -

out you Can't smile with - out you,

Can't laugh and I can't sing, I'm find - in' it hard to

do an - y - thing. You see, I can't smile with -

Bridge Over Troubled Water

Registration 3
Rhythm: Slow Rock or Ballad

Words and Music by
Paul Simon

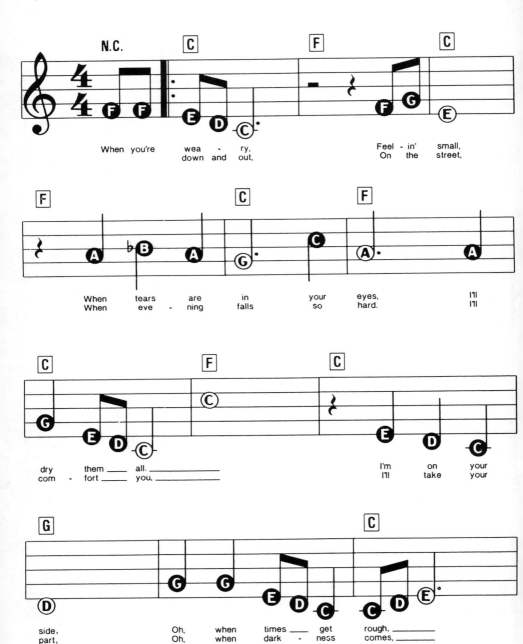

25

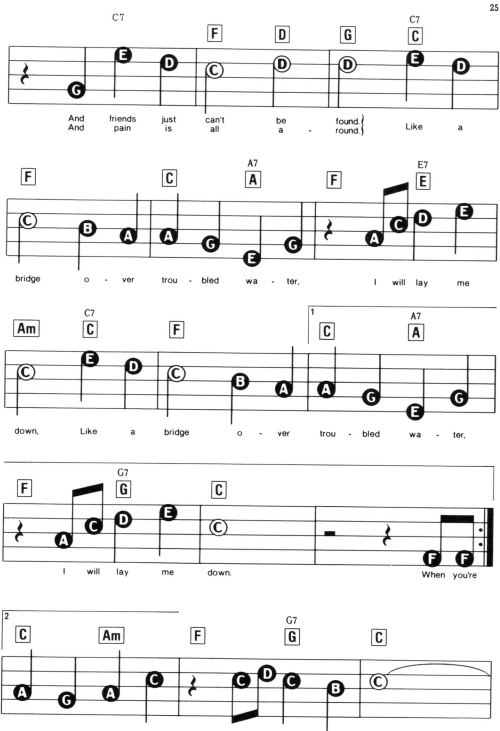

26

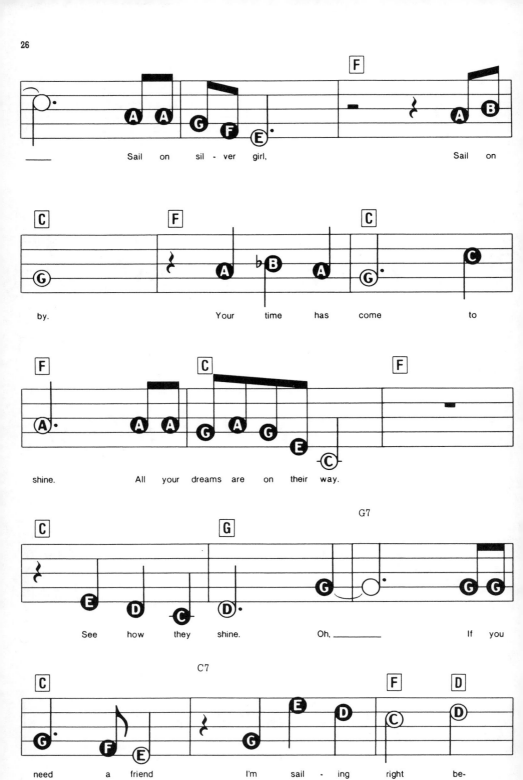

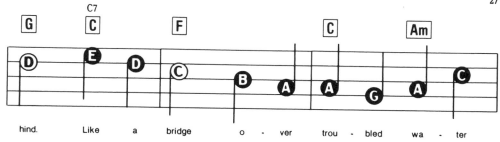

hind. Like a bridge o - ver trou - bled wa - ter

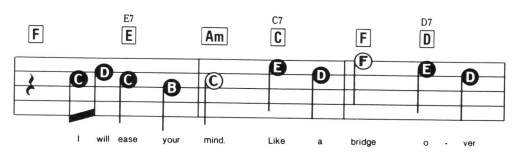

I will ease your mind. Like a bridge o - ver

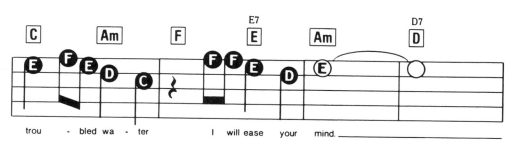

trou - bled wa - ter I will ease your mind.

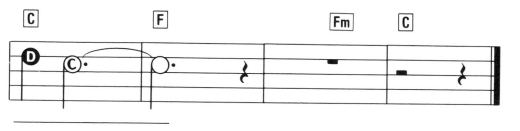

By the Time I Get to Phoenix

Registration 1
Rhythm: Fox Trot or Ballad

Words and Music by
Jimmy Webb

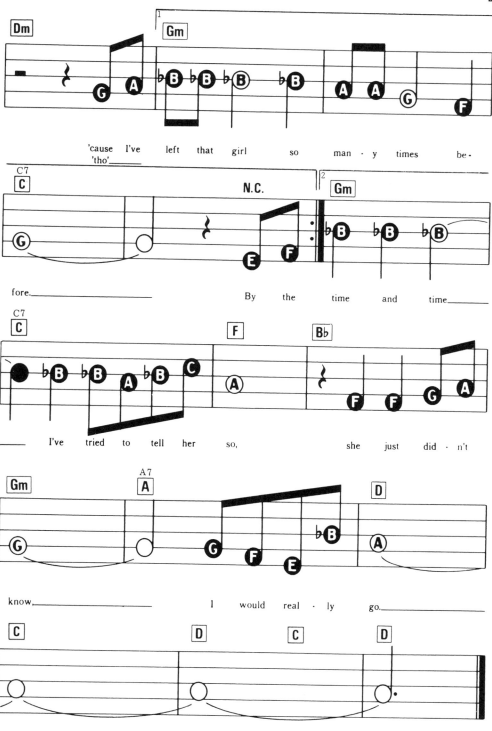

'cause I've left that girl so man · y times be -
'tho'_____

fore._____ By the time and time_____

_____ I've tried to tell her so, she just did · n't

know,_____ I would real · ly go._____

Crying

Registration 4
Rhythm: Ballad or Slow Rock

Words and Music by Roy Orbison
and Joe Melson

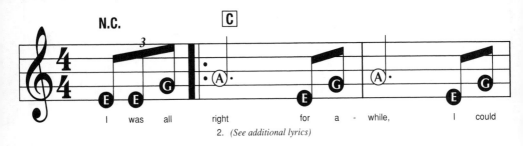

I was all right for a - while, I could

2. *(See additional lyrics)*

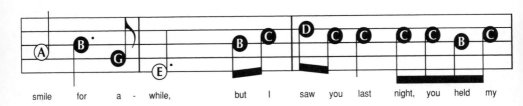

smile for a - while, but I saw you last night, you held my

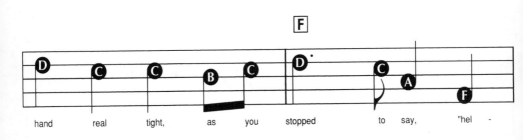

hand real tight, as you stopped to say, "hel -

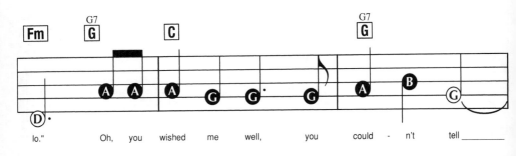

lo." Oh, you wished me well, you could - n't tell

31

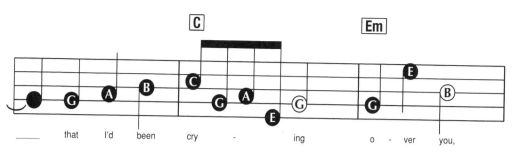

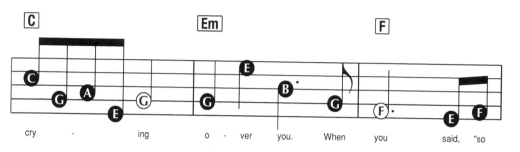

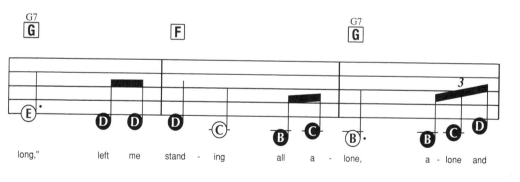

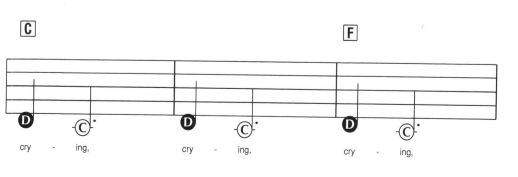

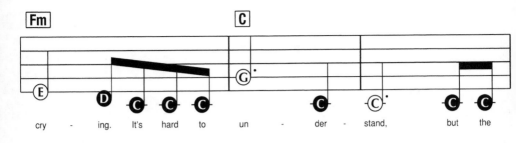

cry - ing. It's hard to un - der - stand, but the

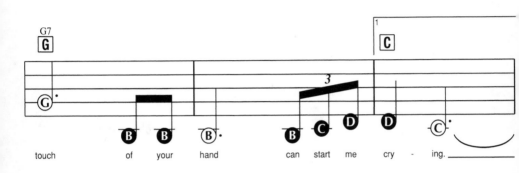

touch of your hand can start me cry - ing. _____

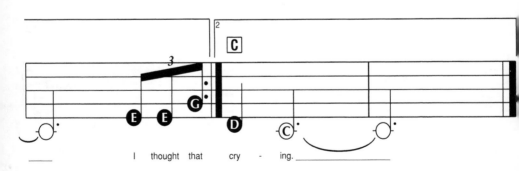

_____ I thought that cry - ing. _____

Additional Lyrics

2   I thought that I was over you,
    But it's true, so true:
    I love you even more than I did before.
    But darling, what can I do?
    For you don't love me and I'll always be
    Crying over you, crying over you.
    Yes, now you're gone and from this moment on
    I'll be crying, crying, crying, crying,
    Yeah, crying, crying over you.

Daniel

Registration 2
Rhythm: Latin or Rock

Words and Music by Elton John
and Bernie Taupin

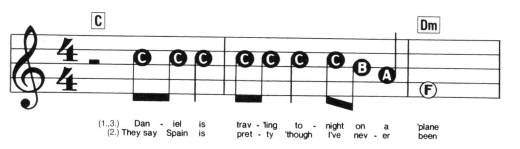

(1.,3.) Dan - iel is trav - 'ling to - night on a 'plane
(2.) They say Spain is pret - ty 'though I've nev - er been

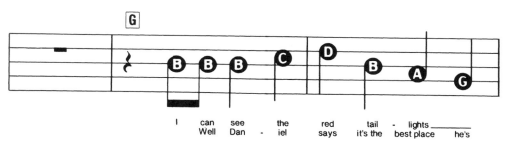

I can see the red tail - lights _____
Well Dan - iel says it's the best place he's

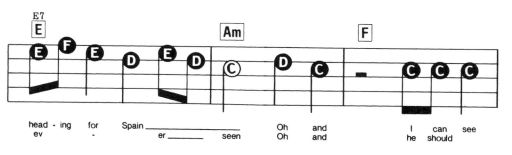

head - ing for Spain _____
ev - er _____ seen

Oh and
Oh and

I can see
he should

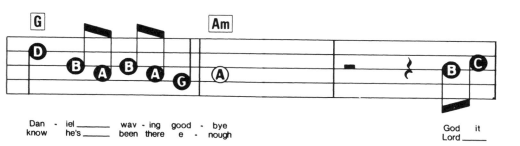

Dan - iel _____ wav - ing good - bye
know he's _____ been there e - nough

God it
Lord _____

34

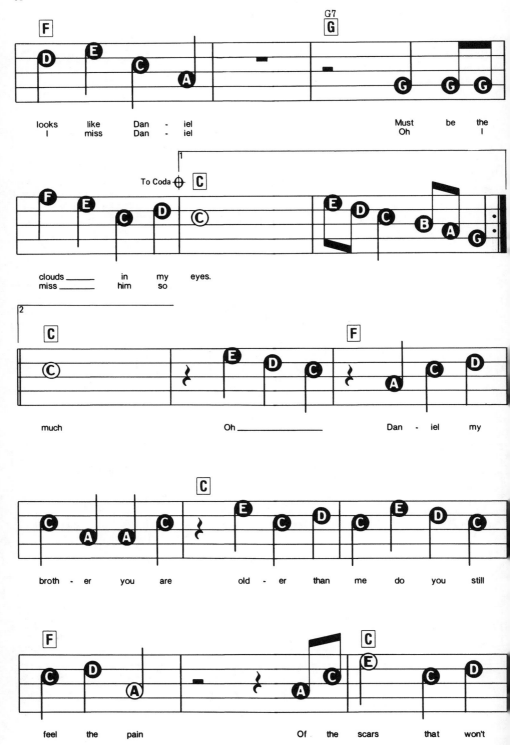

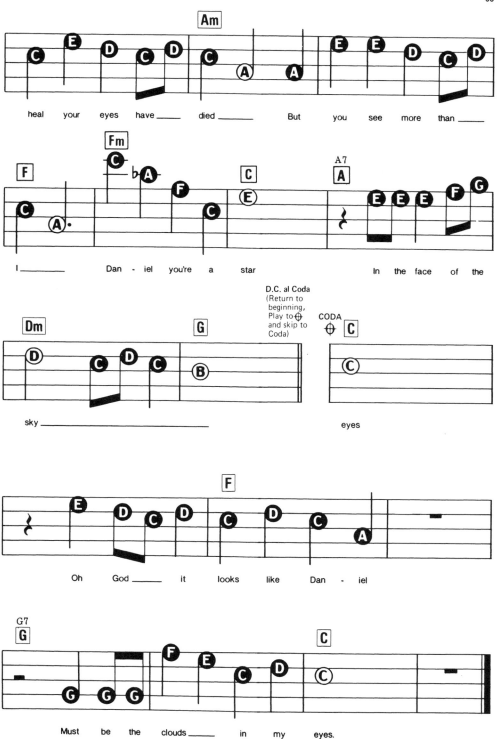

Daydream

Registration 5
Rhythm: Swing

Words and Music by
John Sebastian

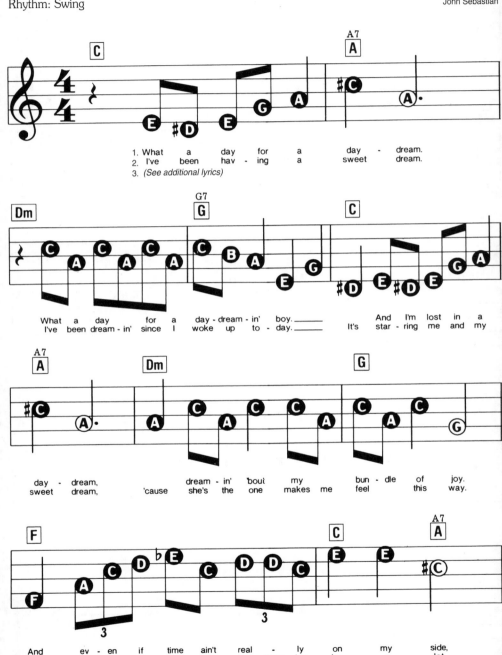

1. What a day for a day - dream.
2. I've been hav - ing a sweet dream.
3. *(See additional lyrics)*

What a day for a day - dream - in' boy._____ And I'm lost in a
I've been dream - in' since I woke up to - day._____ It's star - ring me and my

day - dream, dream - in' 'bout my bun - dle of joy.
sweet dream, 'cause she's the one makes me feel this way.

And ev - en if time ain't real - ly on my side,
And ev - en if time is pass - ing by a lot,

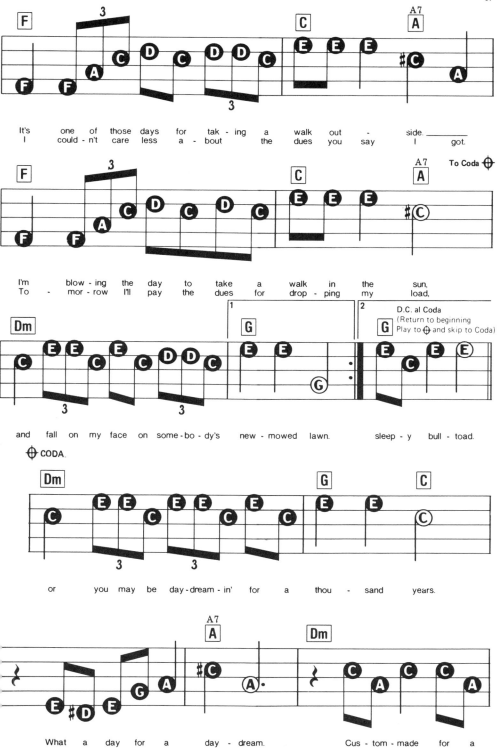

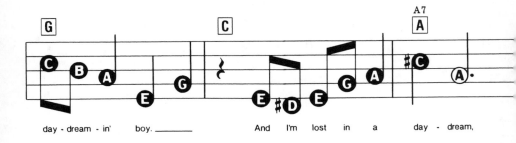

day - dream - in' boy. _____ And I'm lost in a day - dream,

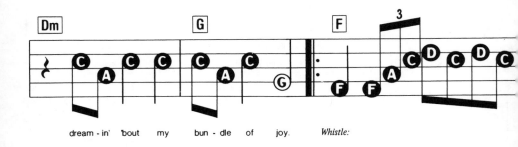

dream - in' 'bout my bun - dle of joy. *Whistle:*

Repeat and Fade

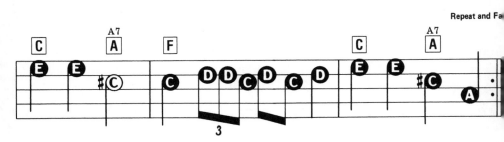

Additional Lyrics

Verse 3. (Whistle) Whistle Whistle Whistle

And you can be sure that if you're feelin' right,
A Daydream will last till long into the night.
Tomorrow at breakfast you may pick up your ears,
Or you may be daydreamin' for a thousand years.

Evergreen

Registration 3
Rhythm: Slow Rock or Ballad

Words by Paul Williams
Music by Barbra Streisand

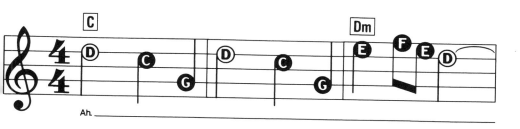

Ah.

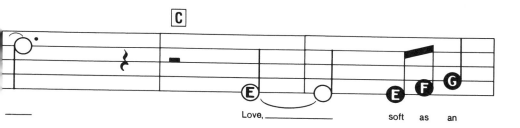

Love, _____ soft as an

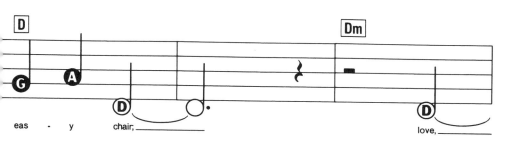

eas - y chair; _____ love, _____

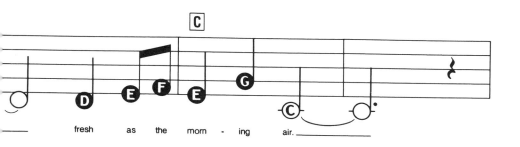

fresh as the morn - ing air. _____

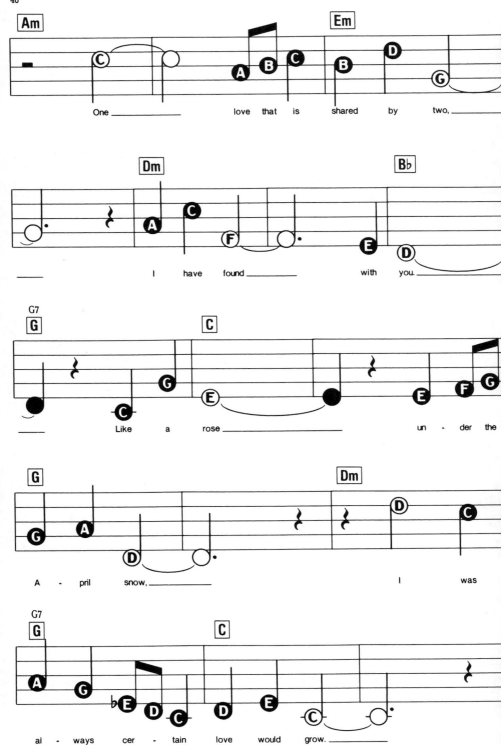

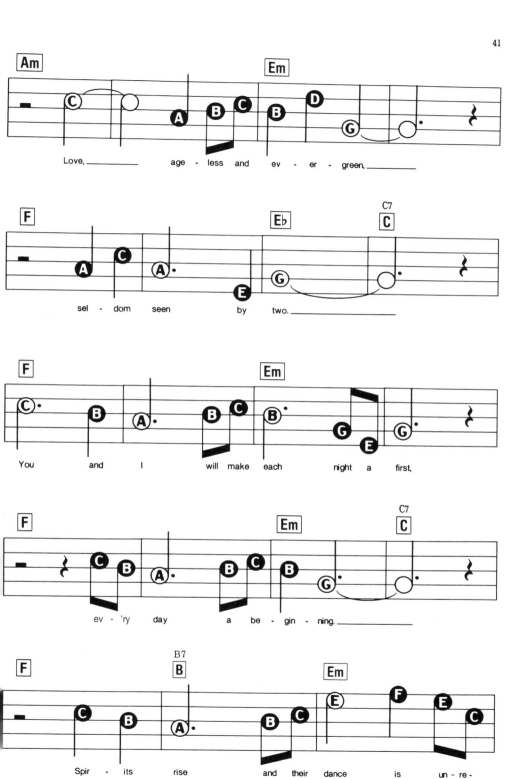

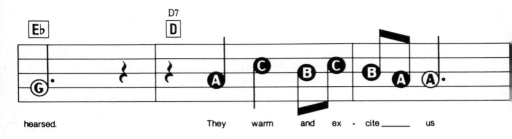

hearsed.   They   warm   and   ex - cite _____ us

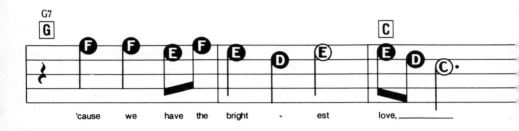

'cause   we   have   the   bright - est   love, _____

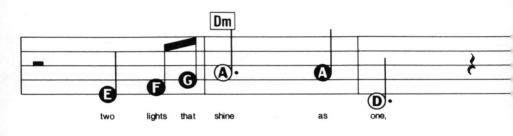

two   lights   that   shine   as   one,

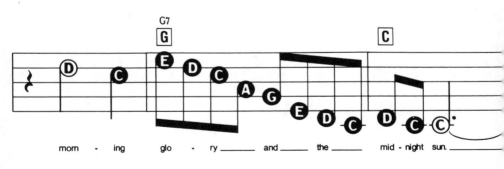

morn - ing   glo - ry _____ and _____ the _____ mid - night sun. _____

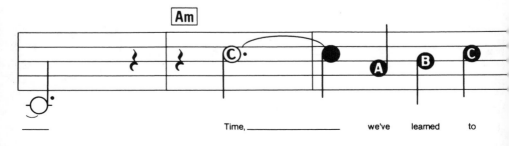

_____   Time, _____ we've   learned   to

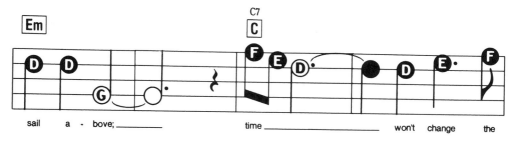

sail a - bove; _____ time _____ won't change the

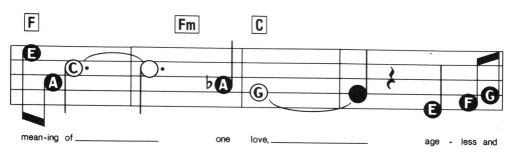

mean-ing of _____ one love, _____ age - less and

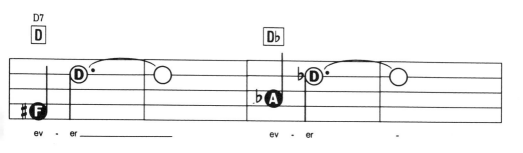

ev - er _____ ev - er -

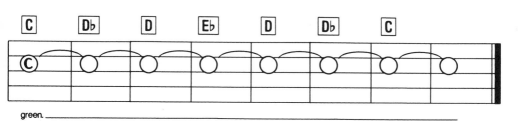

green. _____

Don't Let the Sun Go Down on Me

Registration 8
Rhythm: Ballad

Words and Music by Elton John
and Bernie Taupin

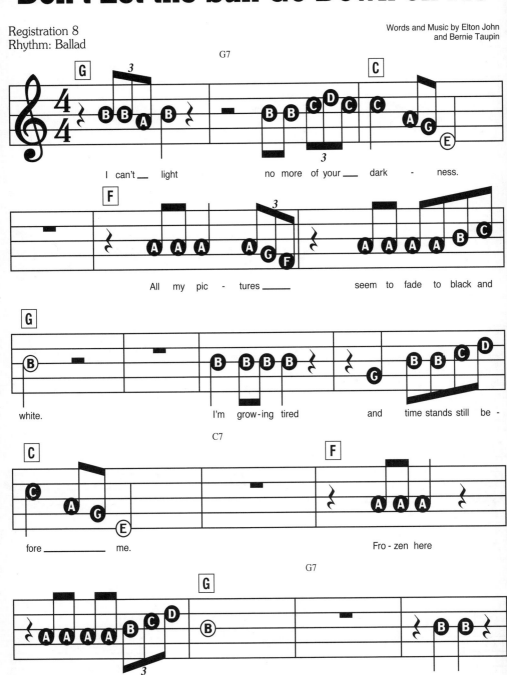

I can't __ light no more of your __ dark - ness.

All my pic - tures _____ seem to fade to black and

white. I'm grow - ing tired and time stands still be -

fore _____ me. Fro - zen here

on the lad - der of my __ life. Too late

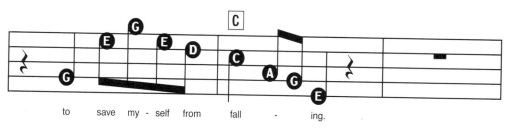

to save my - self from fall - ing.

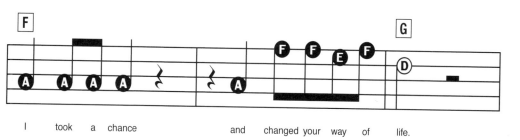

I took a chance and changed your way of life.

G7

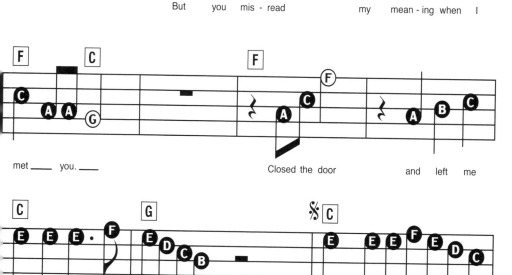

But you mis - read my mean - ing when I

met ____ you. ____

Closed the door and left me

blind - ed by the light. ____

Don't let the sun ____ go

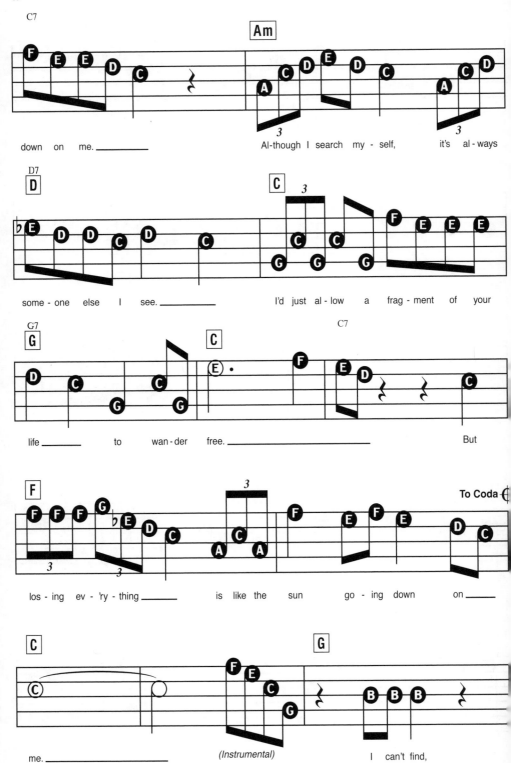

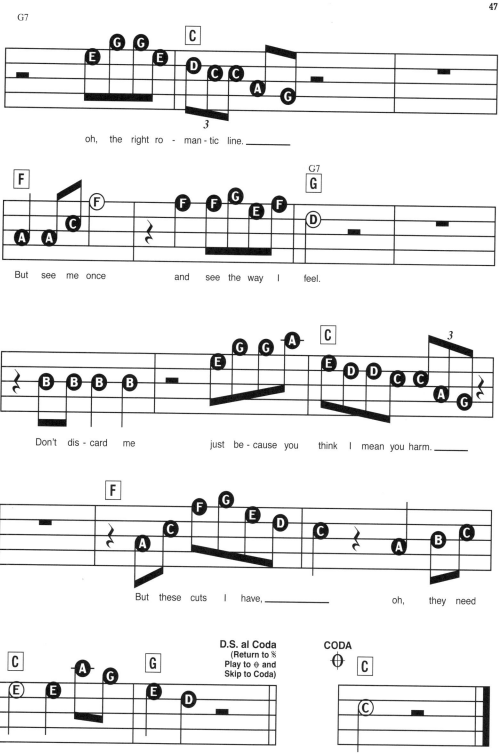

oh, the right ro - man - tic line. _____

But see me once and see the way I feel.

Don't dis - card me just be - cause you think I mean you harm. _____

But these cuts I have, _____ oh, they need

D.S. al Coda
(Return to 𝄋
Play to ⊕ and
Skip to Coda)

CODA

love to help them heal. _____

me.

Dust in the Wind

Registration 4
Rhythm: Rock

Words and Music by
Kerry Livgren

49

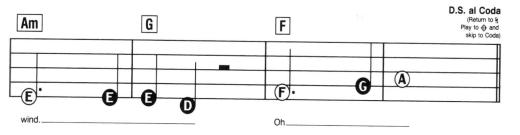

wind._____ Oh_____

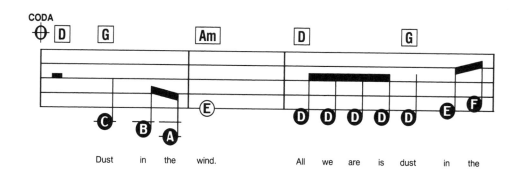

Dust in the wind. All we are is dust in the

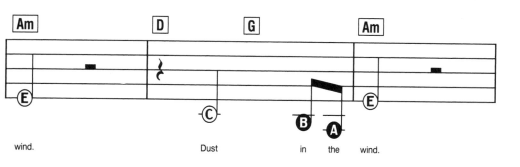

wind. Dust in the wind.

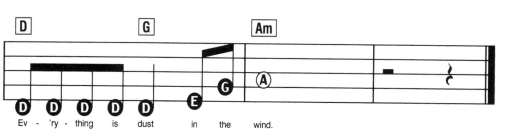

Ev - 'ry - thing is dust in the wind.

Every Breath You Take

Registration 1
Rhythm: Rock or 8-Beat

Words and Music by
Sting

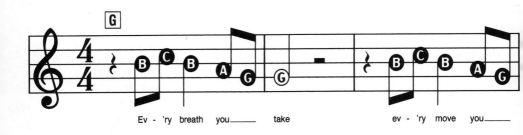

Ev - 'ry breath you take   ev - 'ry move you

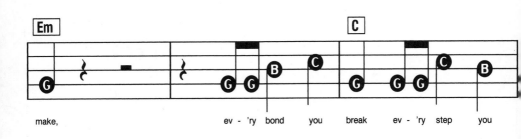

make,   ev - 'ry bond you break   ev - 'ry step you

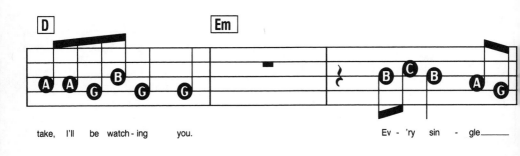

take, I'll be watch - ing you.   Ev - 'ry sin - gle

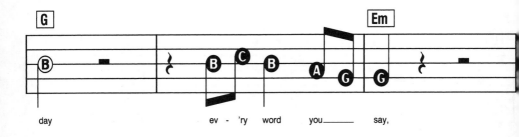

day   ev - 'ry word you   say,

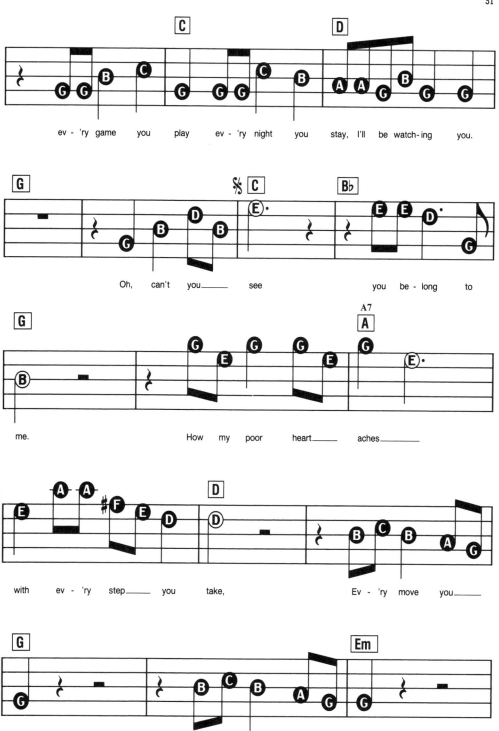

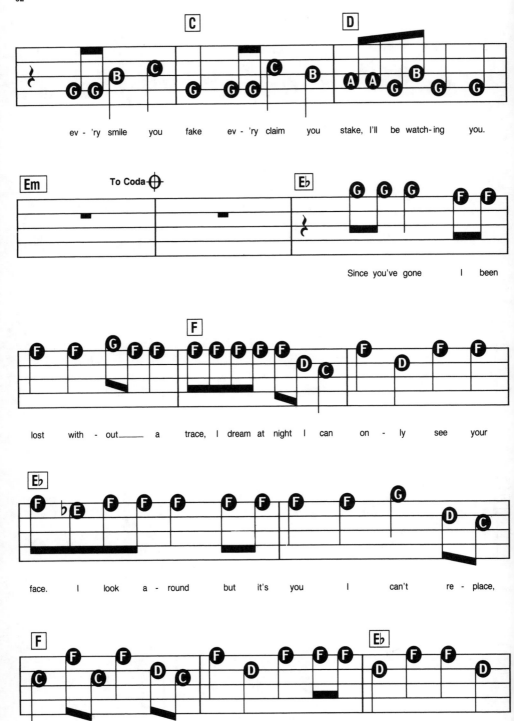

ev - 'ry smile you fake ev - 'ry claim you stake, I'll be watch-ing you.

Since you've gone I been

lost with - out_____ a trace, I dream at night I can on - ly see your

face. I look a - round but it's you I can't re - place,

I feel so cold and I long for your em - brace. I keep cry - ing

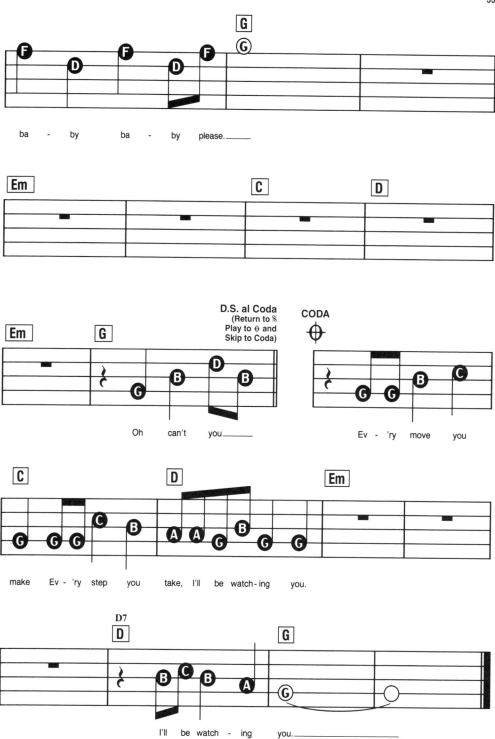

ba - by ba - by please.____

D.S. al Coda
(Return to 𝄋
Play to ⊕ and
Skip to Coda)

CODA

Oh can't you____

Ev - 'ry move you

make Ev - 'ry step you take, I'll be watch-ing you.

I'll be watch - ing you.____

Give a Little Bit

Registration 1
Rhythm: 8-Beat or Rock

Words and Music by Rick Davies
and Roger Hodgson

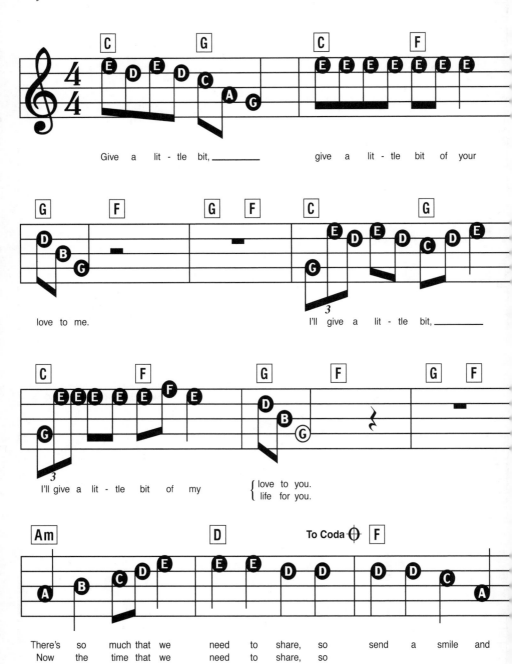

Give a lit - tle bit, _____ give a lit - tle bit of your

love to me. I'll give a lit - tle bit, _____

I'll give a lit - tle bit of my { love to you.
{ life for you.

There's so much that we need to share, so send a smile and
Now the time that we need to share, so

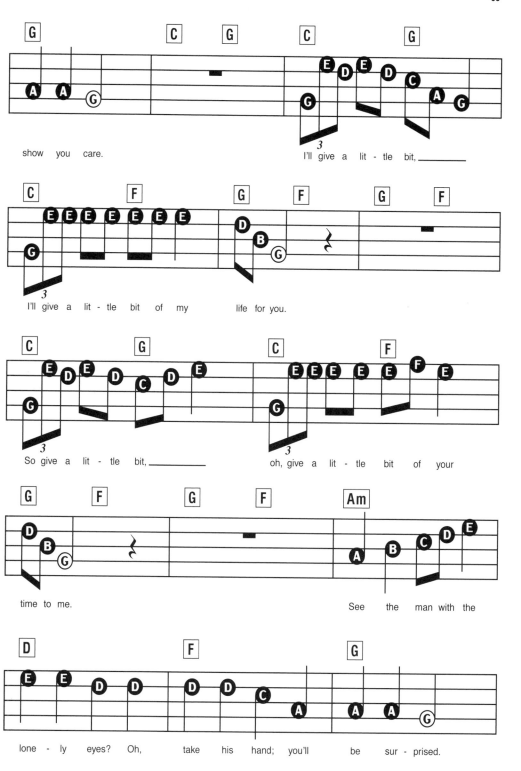

56

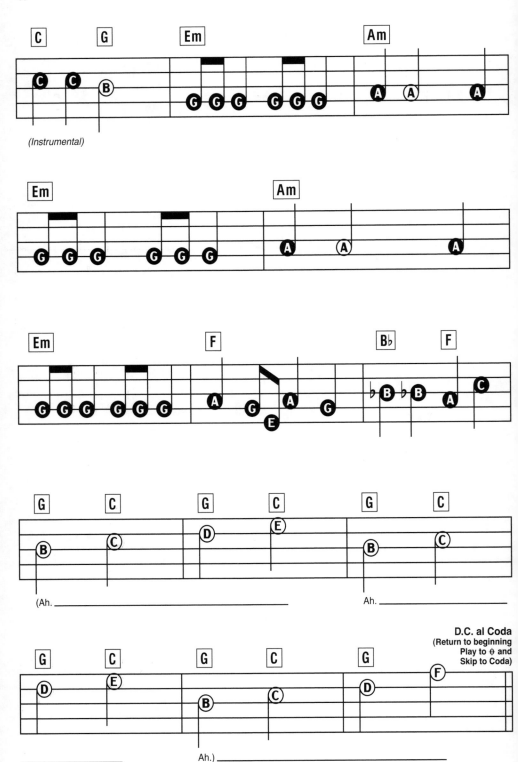

CODA

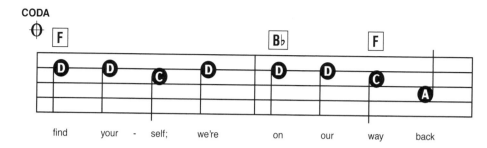

find your - self; we're on our way back

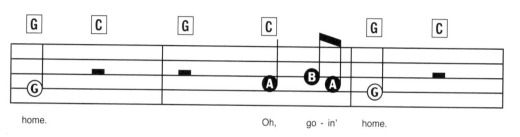

home. Oh, go - in' home.

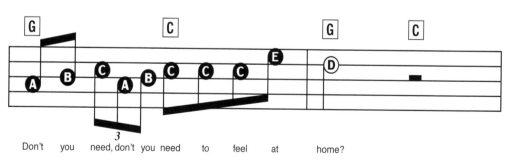

Don't you need, don't you need to feel at home?

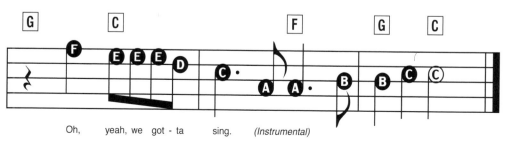

Oh, yeah, we got - ta sing. *(Instrumental)*

Green Green Grass of Home

Registration 2
Rhythm: Country

Words and Music by
Curly Putman

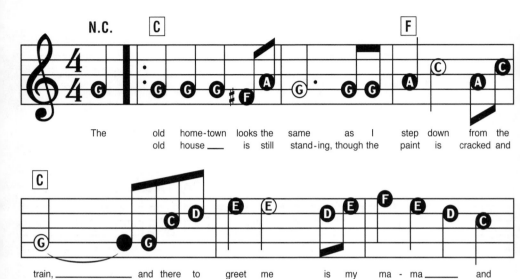

The old home-town looks the same as I step down from the
old house ___ is still stand-ing, though the paint is cracked and

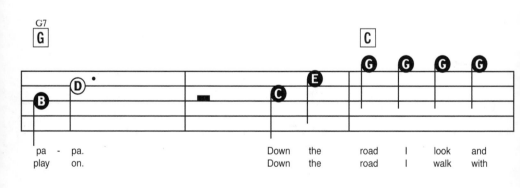

train, _____ and there to greet me is my ma - ma _____ and
dry, _____ and there's that old oak tree _____ that I used _____ to

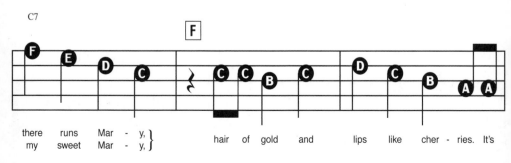

pa - pa. Down the road I look and
play on. Down the road I walk with

there runs Mar - y, } hair of gold and lips like cher - ries. It's
my sweet Mar - y, }

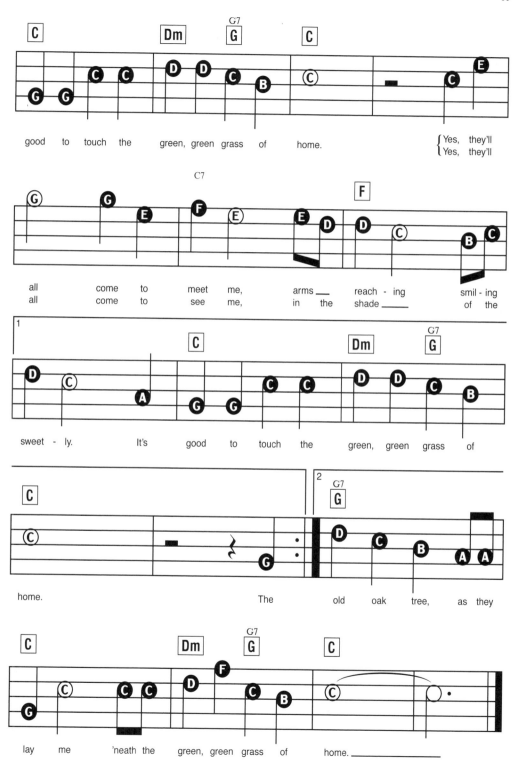

Hallelujah

Registration 4
Rhythm: 6/8 March

Words and Music by
Leonard Cohen

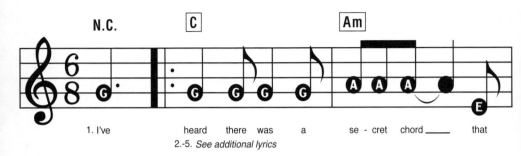

1. I've   heard   there   was   a   se - cret   chord _____ that

2.-5. *See additional lyrics*

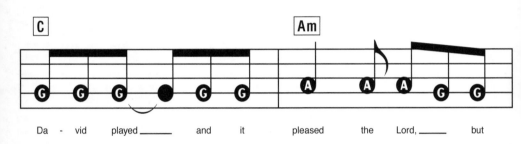

Da - vid   played _____ and   it   pleased   the   Lord, _____ but

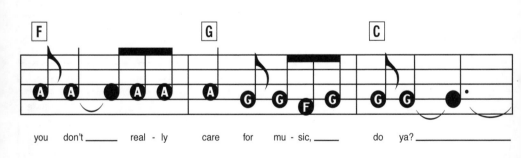

you   don't _____ real - ly   care   for   mu - sic, _____ do   ya? _____

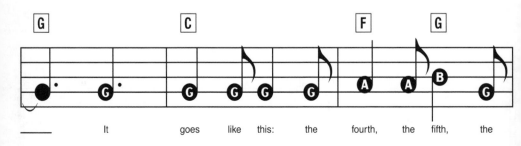

_____ It   goes   like   this: the   fourth,   the   fifth,   the

61

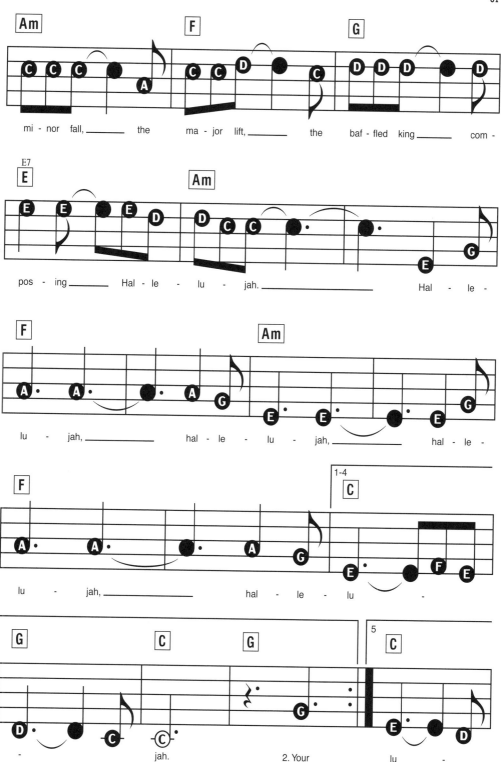

62

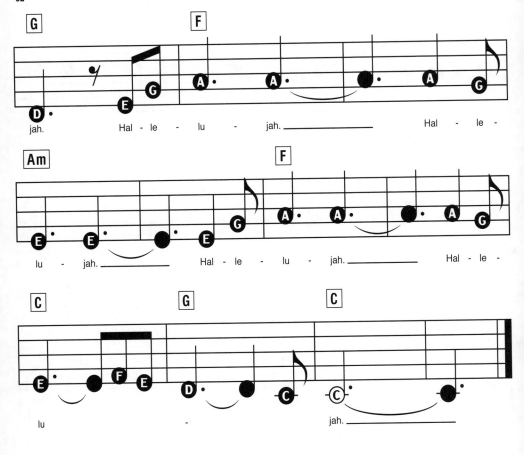

jah.   Hal - le - lu - jah. _____   Hal - le -

lu - jah. _____   Hal - le - lu - jah. _____   Hal - le -

lu -   jah. _____

Additional Lyrics

2. Your faith was strong but you needed proof.
   You saw her bathing on the roof.
   Her beauty and the moonlight overthrew ya.
   She tied you to a kitchen chair.
   She broke your throne, she cut your hair.
   And from your lips she drew the Hallelujah.

3. Maybe I have been here before.
   I know this room, I've walked this floor.
   I used to live alone before I knew ya.
   I've seen your flag on the marble arch.
   Love is not a vict'ry march.
   It's a cold and it's a broken Hallelujah.

4. There was a time you let me know
   What's real and going on below.
   But now you never show it to me, do ya?
   And remember when I moved in you.
   The holy dark was movin', too,
   And every breath we drew was Hallelujah.

5. Maybe there's a God above,
   And all I ever learned from love
   Was how to shoot at someone who outdrew ya.
   And it's not a cry you can hear at night.
   It's not somebody who's seen the light.
   It's a cold and it's a broken Hallelujah.

A Groovy Kind of Love

Registration 5
Rhythm: 8-Beat or Rock

Words and Music by Toni Wine
and Carole Bayer Sager

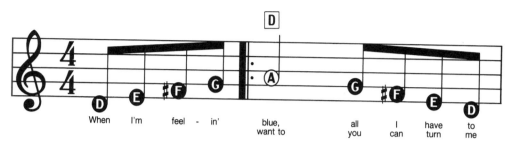

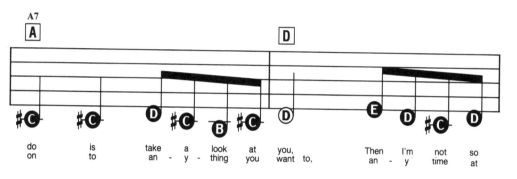

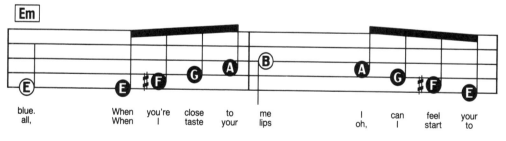

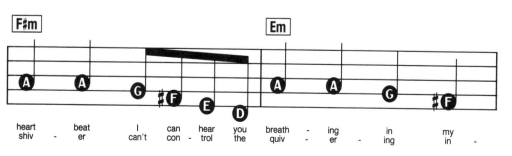

64

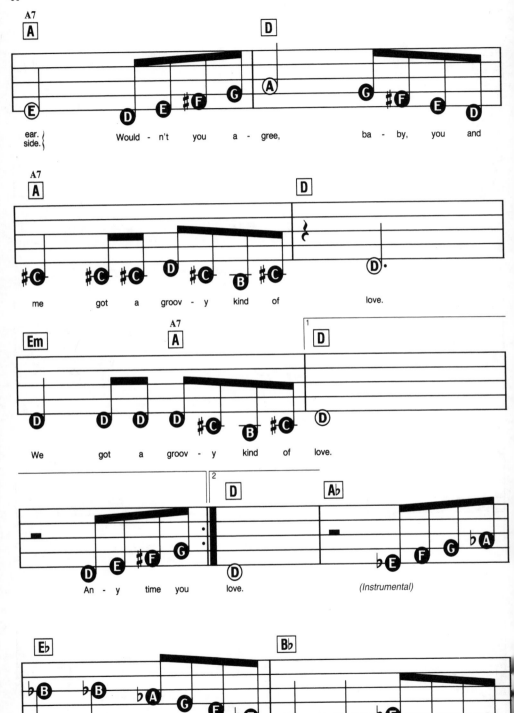

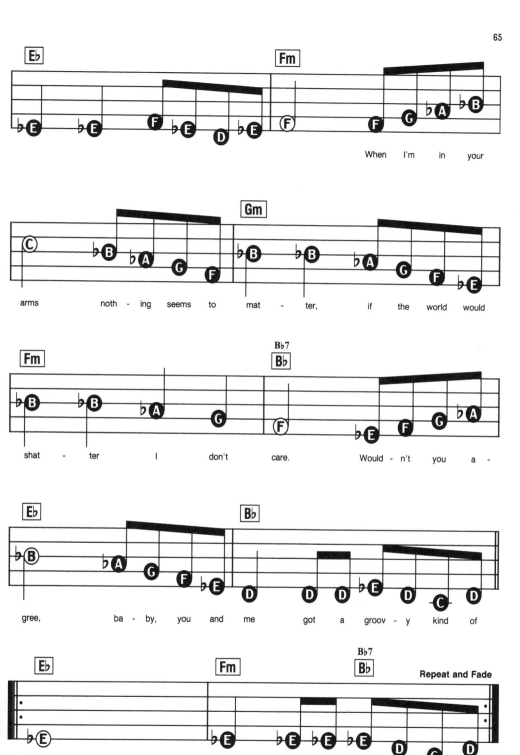

Hello

Registration 1
Rhythm: Slow Rock or Ballad

Words and Music by
Lionel Richie

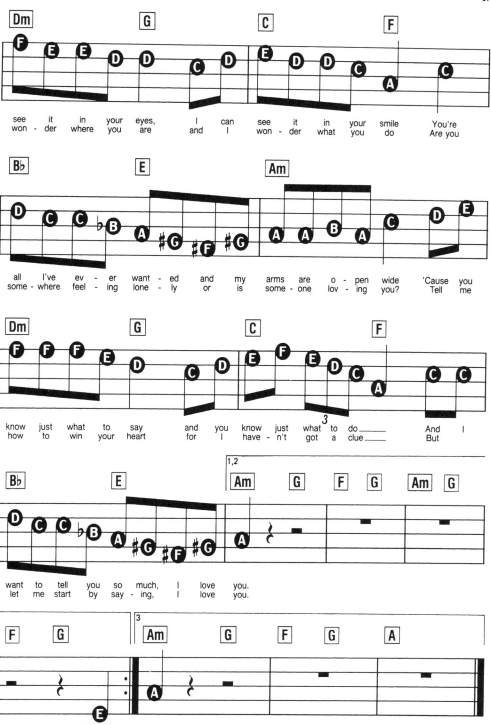

Hello, It's Me

Registration 1
Rhythm: Ballad

Words and Music by
Todd Rundgren

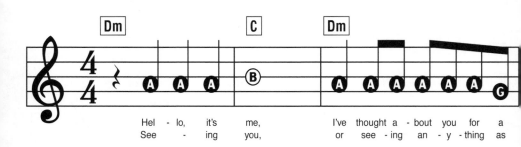

Hel - lo, it's me, I've thought a - bout you for a
See - ing you, or see - ing an - y - thing as

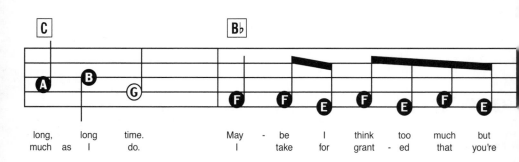

long, long time. May - be I think too much but
much as I do. I take for grant - ed that you're

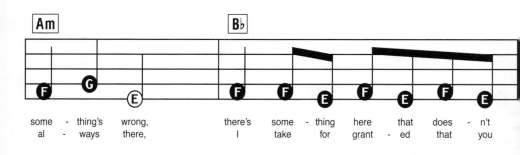

some - thing's wrong, there's some - thing here that does - n't
al - ways there, I take for grant - ed that you

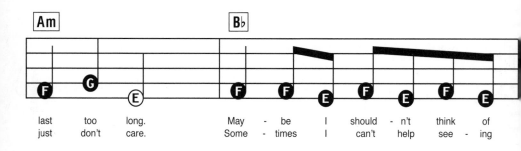

last too long. May - be I should - n't think of
just don't care. Some - times I can't help see - ing

69

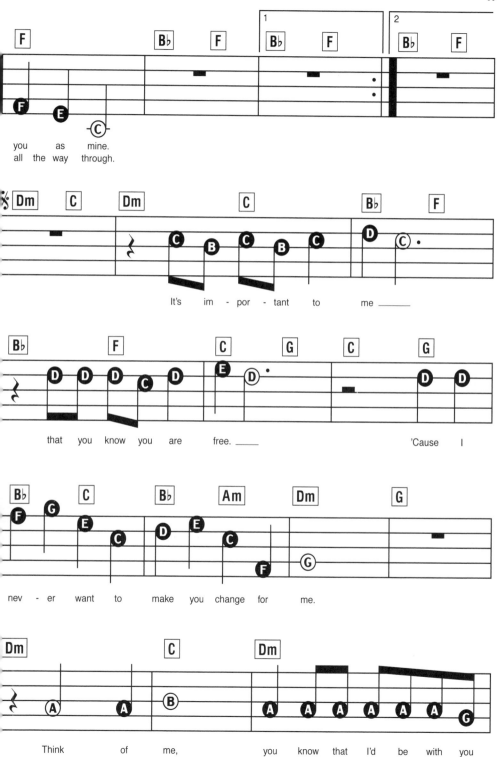

70

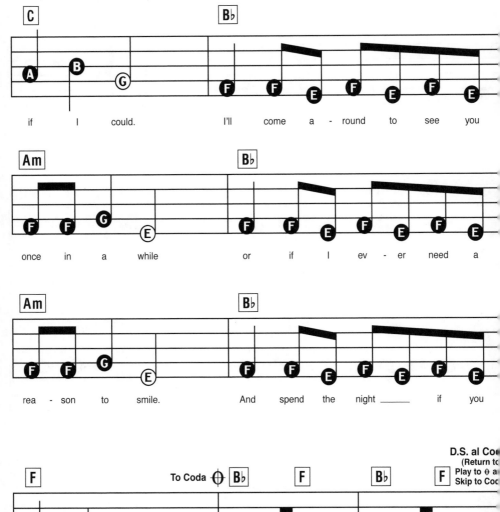

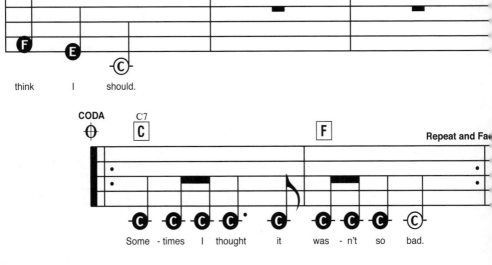

Holding Back the Years

Registration 7
Rhythm: Rock

Words by Mick Hucknall
Music by Mick Hucknall and Neil Moss

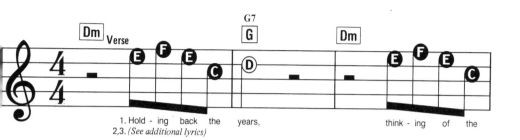

1. Hold - ing back the years, think - ing of the
2,3. *(See additional lyrics)*

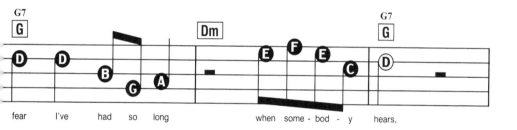

fear I've had so long when some - bod - y hears,

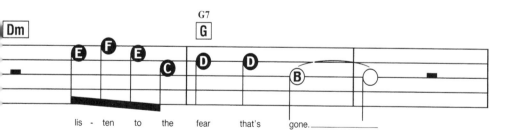

lis - ten to the fear that's gone.___

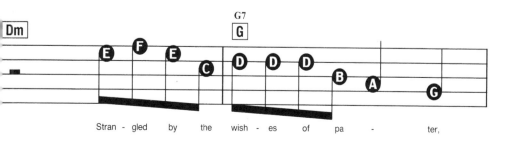

Stran - gled by the wish - es of pa - ter,

72

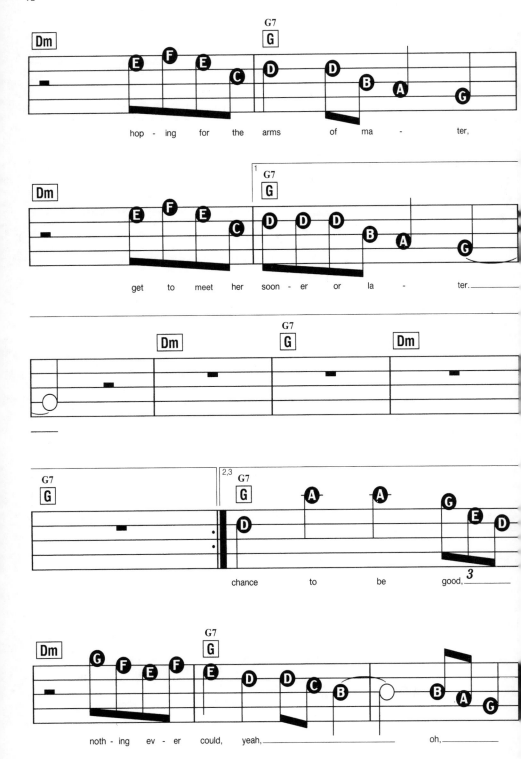

Chorus

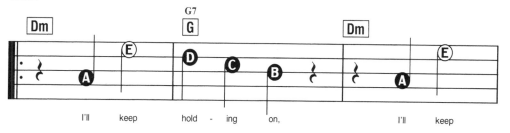

I'll   keep   hold - ing   on,   I'll   keep

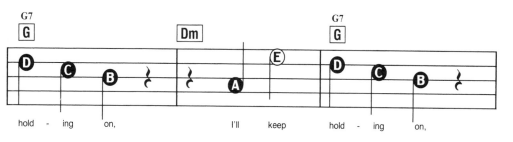

hold - ing   on,   I'll   keep   hold - ing   on,

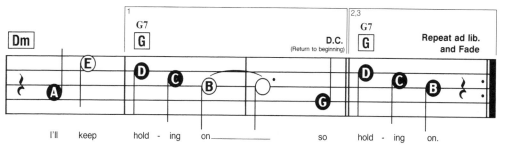

I'll   keep   hold - ing   on_____   so   hold - ing   on.

Additional Lyrics

Verse 2:
Holding back the years,
Chance for me escape from all I've known.
Holding back the tears,
'Cause nothing here has grown.

I've wasted all my tears,
Wasted all those years.
Nothing had the chance to be good,
Nothing ever could.

Verse 3:
(First 9 bars instrumental solo)
Well I've wasted all my tears,
Wasted all of those years.
And nothing had a chance to be good,
'Cause nothing ever could.

A Horse with No Name

Registration 10
Rhythm: Rock or Slow Rock

Words and Music by
Dewey Bunnell

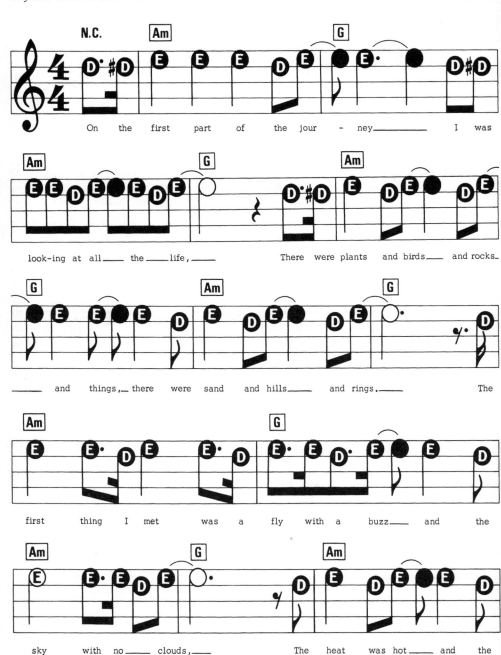

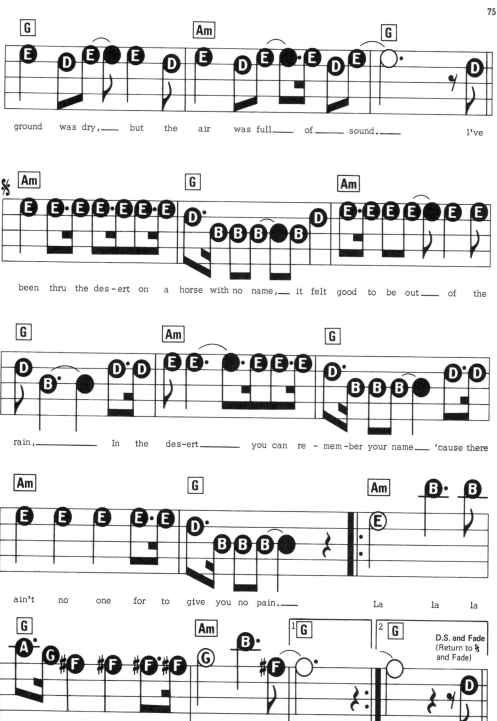

ground was dry,___ but the air was full___ of ___ sound.___ I've

been thru the des-ert on a horse with no name,___ it felt good to be out___ of the

rain,_____ In the des-ert_____ you can re - mem-ber your name___ 'cause there

ain't no one for to give you no pain.___ La la la

la la la la la la la la la._____ ___ I've

D.S. and Fade
(Return to ℅
and Fade)

Hotel California

Registration 9
Rhythm: Rock or Disco

Words and Music by Don Henley,
Glenn Frey and Don Felder

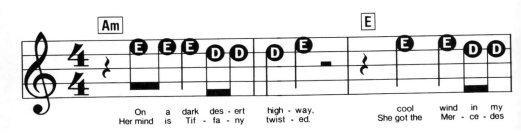

On a dark des - ert high - way,   cool wind in my
Her mind is Tif - fa - ny twist - ed.   She got the Mer - ce - des

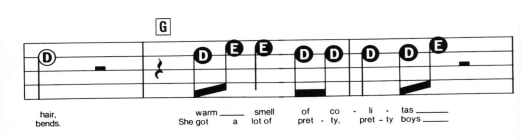

hair,   warm _____ smell of co - li - tas _____
bends.   She got a lot of pret - ty, pret - ty boys _____

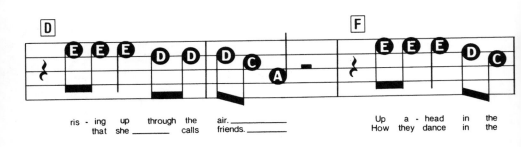

ris - ing up through the air. _____   Up a - head in the
that she _____ calls friends. _____   How they dance in the

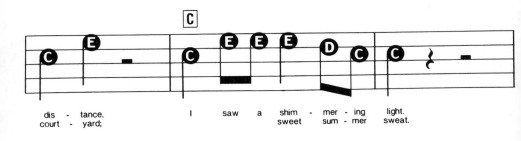

dis - tance,   I saw a shim - mer - ing light.
court - yard;   sweet sum - mer sweat.

77

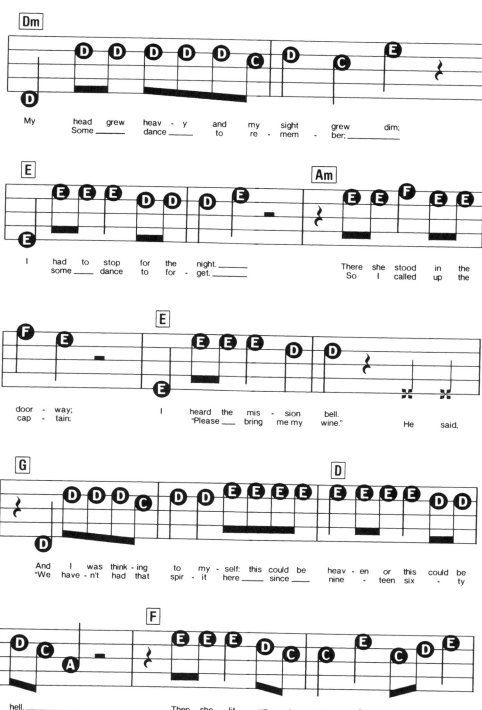

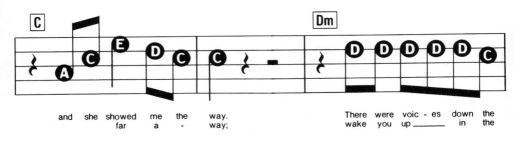

and she showed me the way.
far a - way;
There were voic - es down the
wake you up _____ in the

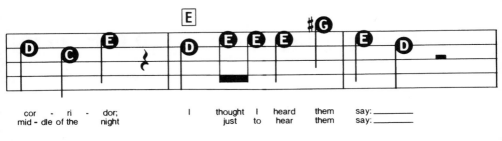

cor - ri - dor;
mid - dle of the night
I thought I heard them say: _____
just to hear them say: _____

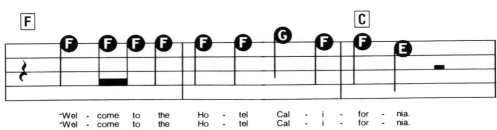

"Wel - come to the Ho - tel Cal - i - for - nia.
"Wel - come to the Ho - tel Cal - i - for - nia.

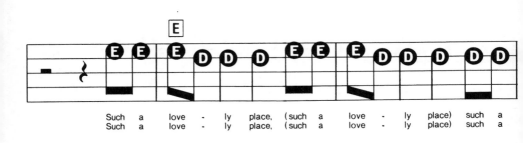

Such a love - ly place, (such a love - ly place) such a
Such a love - ly place, (such a love - ly place) such a

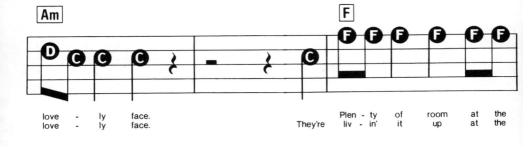

love - ly face.
love - ly face.
They're
Plen - ty of room at the
liv - in' it up at the

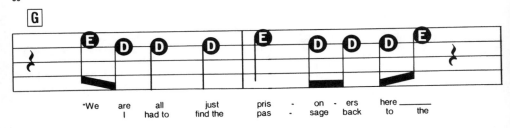

G

"We are all just pris - on - ers here _____ the
I had to find the pas - sage back to the

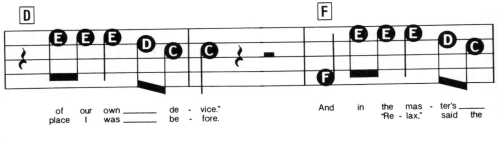

D   F

of our own _____ de - vice."   And in the mas - ter's _____
place I was _____ be - fore.   "Re - lax," said the

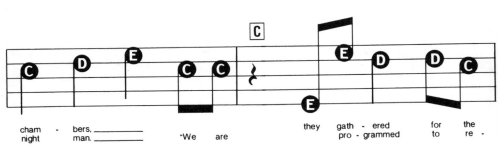

C

cham - bers, _____   they gath - ered for the
night man. _____   "We are pro - grammed to re -

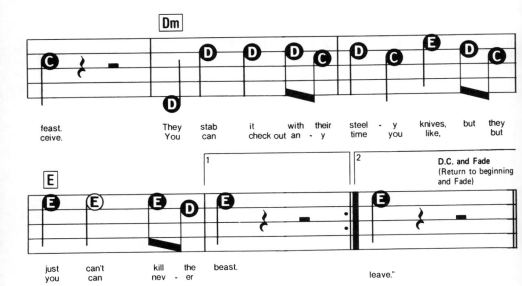

Dm

feast.   They stab it with their steel - y knives, but they
ceive.   You can check out an - y time you like, but

E   1   2   D.C. and Fade
                                              (Return to beginning
                                              and Fade)

just can't kill the beast.
you can nev - er   leave."

I Want to Know What Love Is

Registration 4
Rhythm: Rock or Slow Rock

Words and Music by
Mick Jones

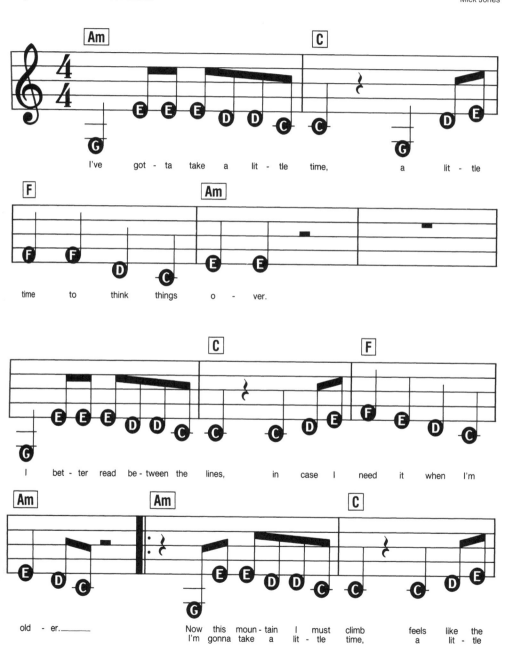

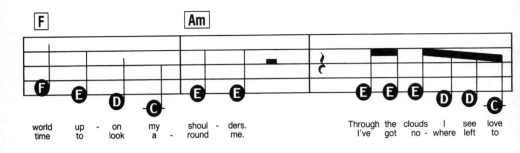

world up - on my shoul - ders.
time to look a - round me.

Through the clouds I see love
I've got no - where left to

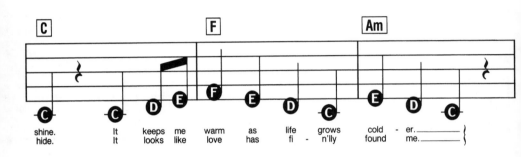

shine. It keeps me warm as life grows cold - er.
hide. It looks like love has fi - n'lly found me.

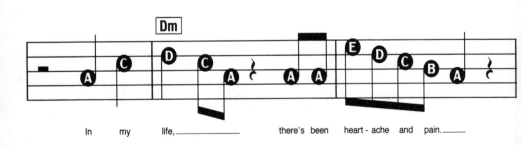

In my life,_____ there's been heart - ache and pain.____

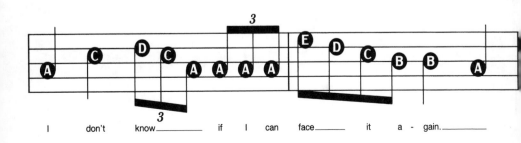

I don't know____ if I can face____ it a - gain.____

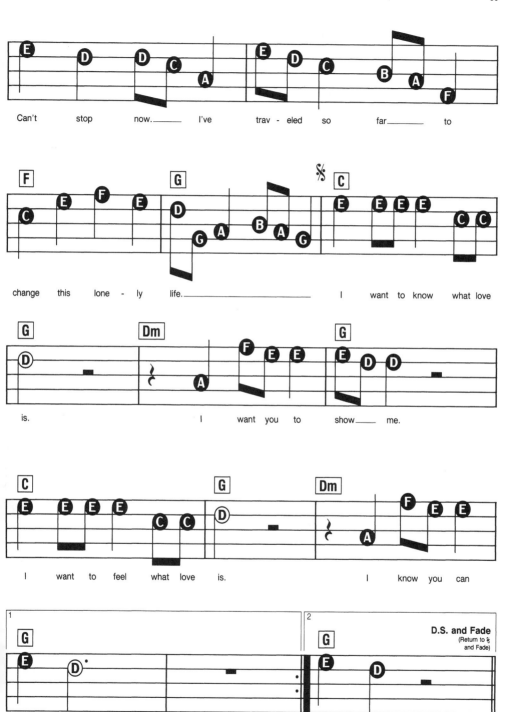

How Much I Feel

Registration 4
Rhythm: Rock

Words and Music by
David Pack

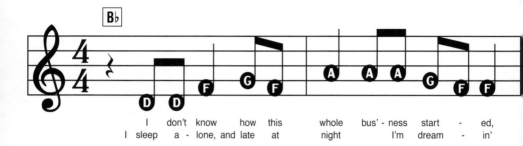

I don't know how this whole bus' - ness start - ed,
I sleep a - lone, and late at night I'm dream - in'

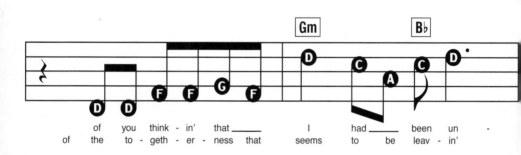

of you think - in' that _____ I had _____ been un -
of the to - geth - er - ness that seems to be leav - in'

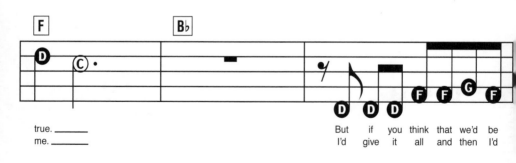

true. _____ But if you think that we'd be
me. _____ I'd give it all and then I'd

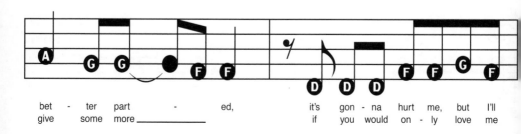

bet - ter part - ed, it's gon - na hurt me, but I'll
give some more _____ if you would on - ly love me

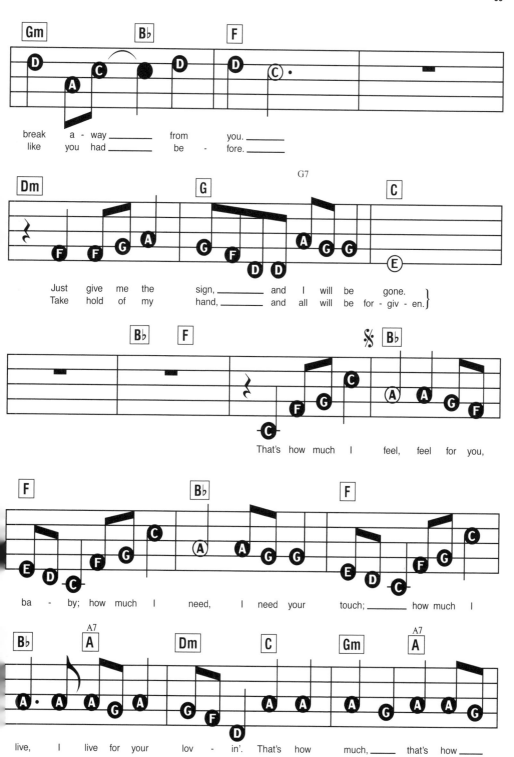

86

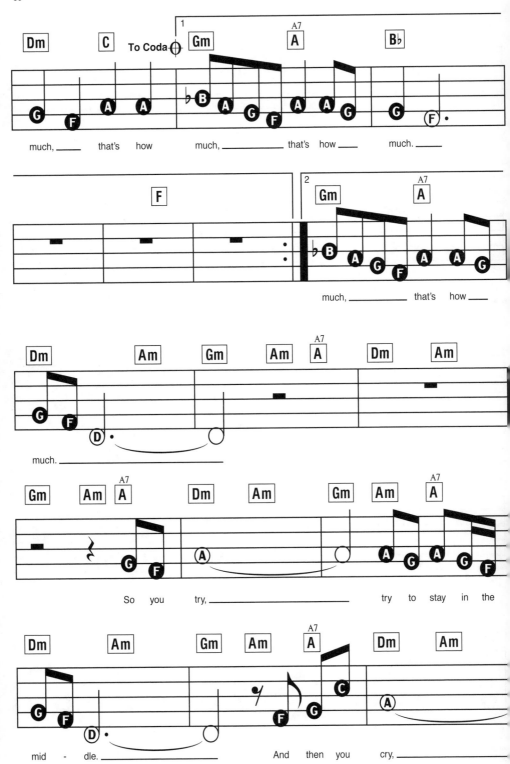

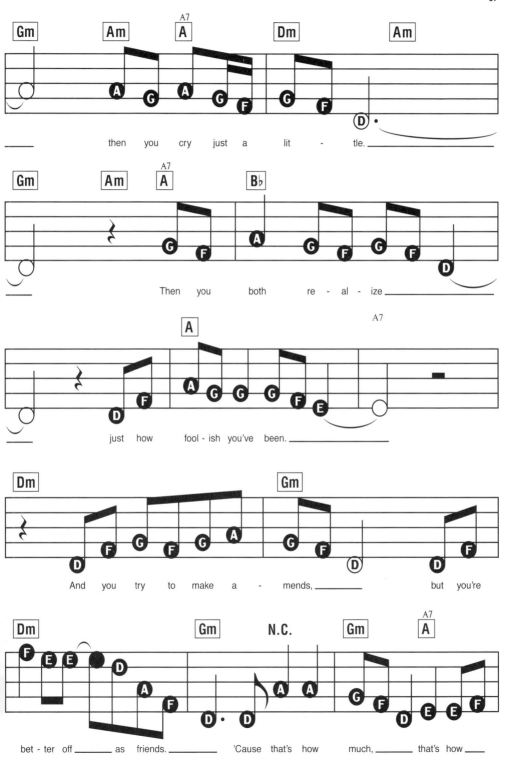

88

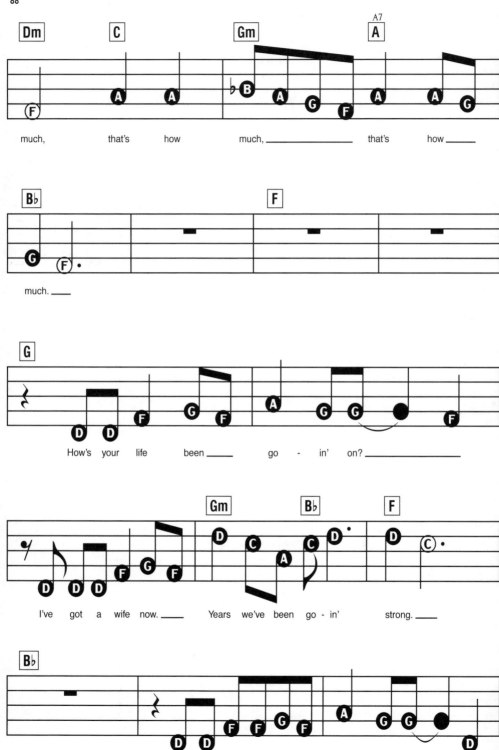

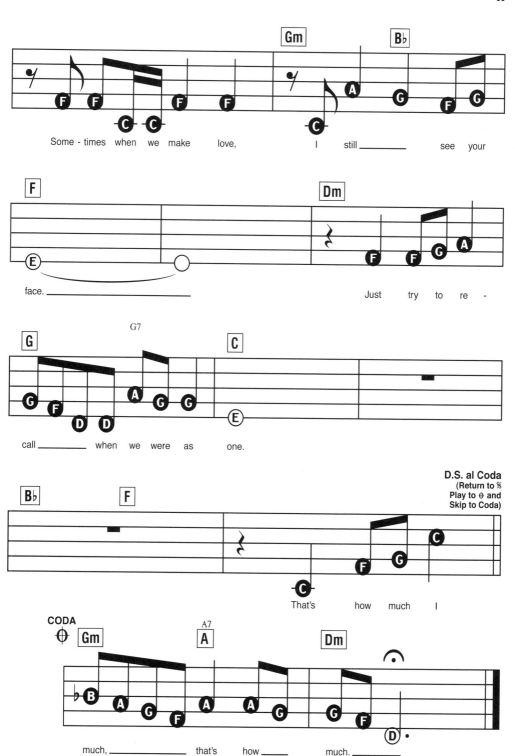

I Will Remember You
Theme from THE BROTHERS McMULLEN

Registration 8
Rhythm: Ballad

Words and Music by Sarah McLachlan,
Seamus Egan and Dave Merenda

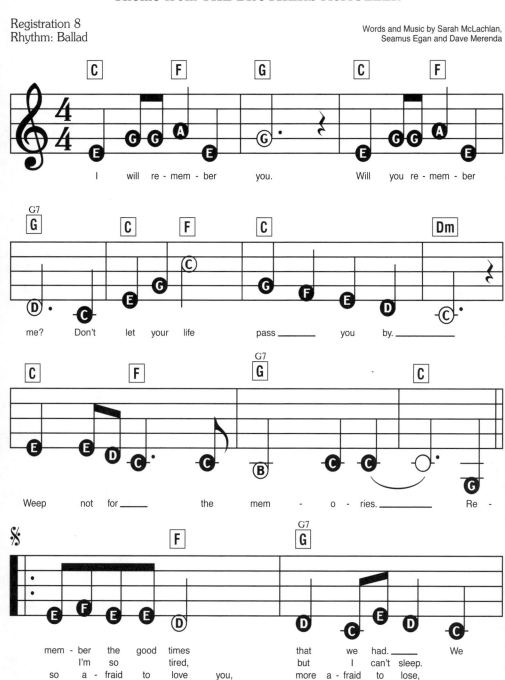

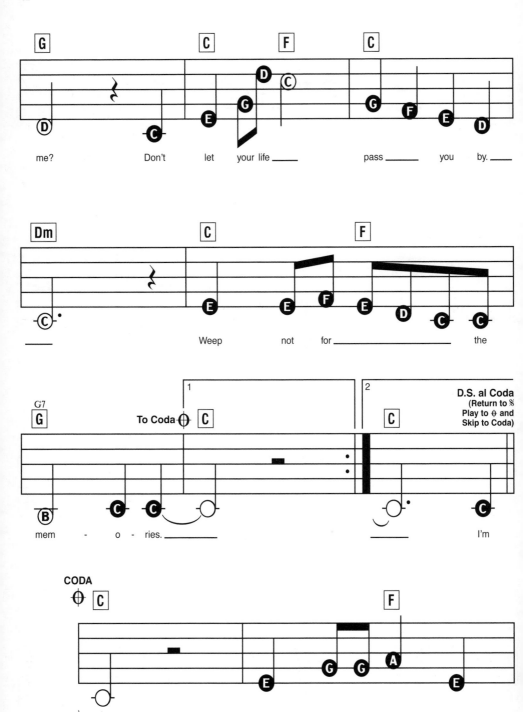

93

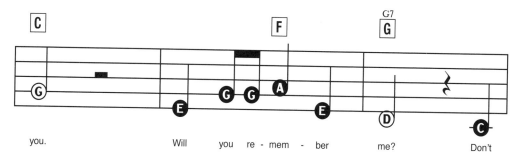

you. Will you re - mem - ber me? Don't

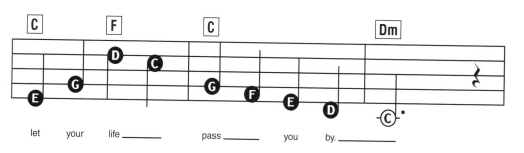

let your life _____ pass _____ you by. _____

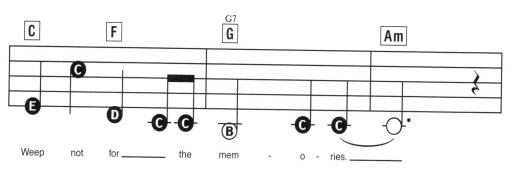

Weep not for _____ the mem - o - ries. _____

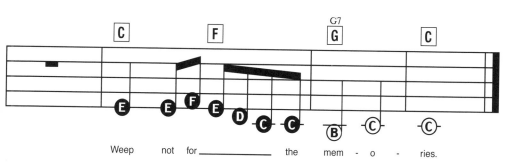

Weep not for _____ the mem - o - ries.

I Write the Songs

Registration 7
Rhythm: Rock or 8-Beat

Words and Music by
Bruce Johnston

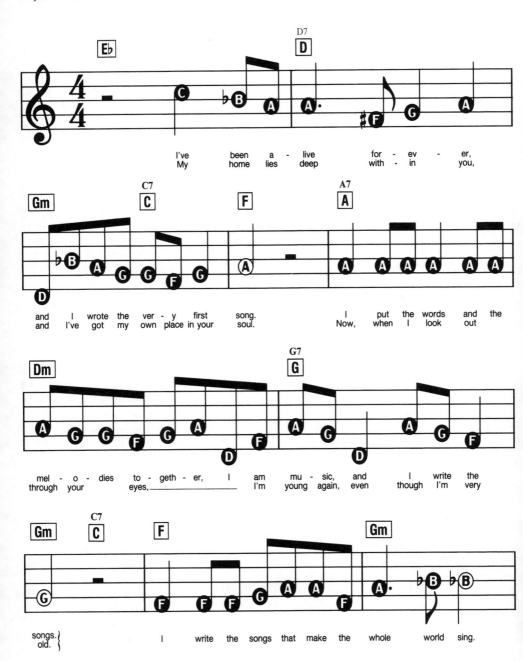

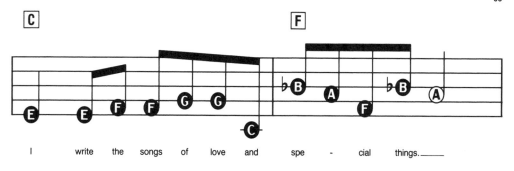

I write the songs of love and spe - cial things.____

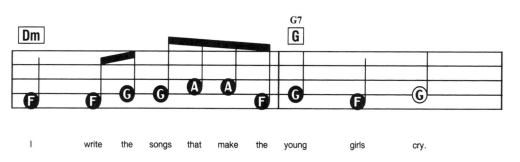

I write the songs that make the young girls cry.

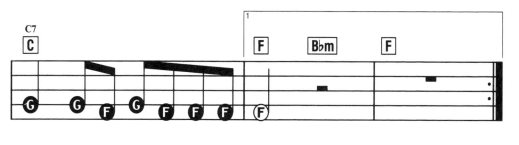

I write the songs, I write the songs.

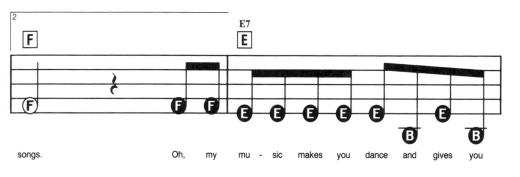

songs. Oh, my mu - sic makes you dance and gives you

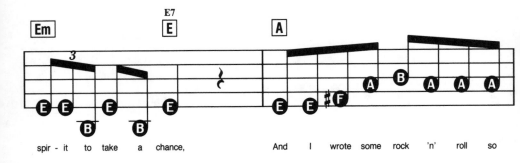

spir - it to take a chance, And I wrote some rock 'n' roll so

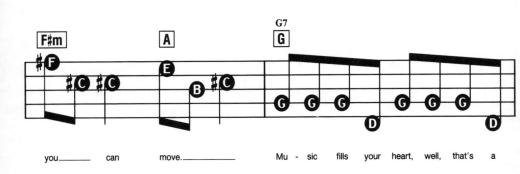

you____ can move._____ Mu - sic fills your heart, well, that's a

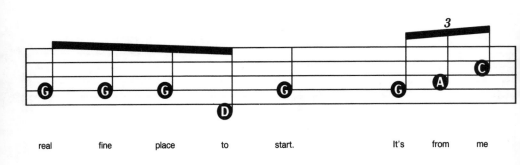

real fine place to start. It's from me

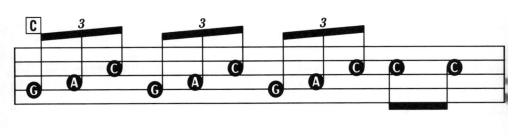

it's for you, it's from you, it's for me, it's a

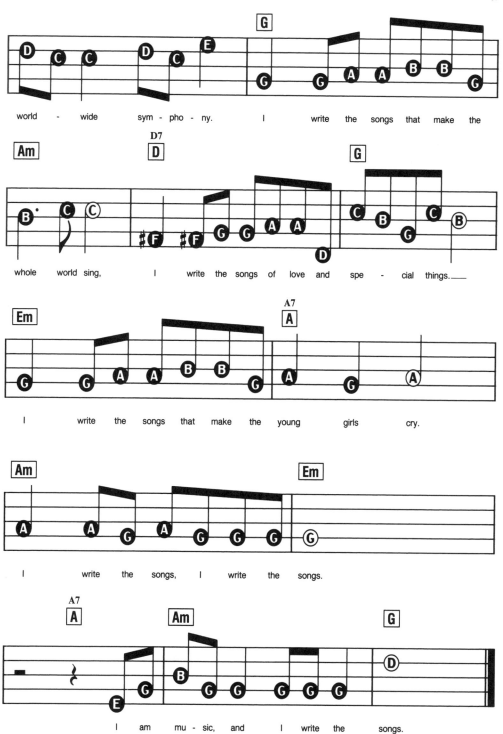

I'd Really Love to See You Tonight

Registration 8
Rhythm: Soft Rock

Words and Music by
Parker McGee

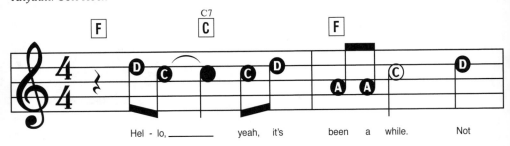

Hel - lo, _____ yeah, it's been a while. Not

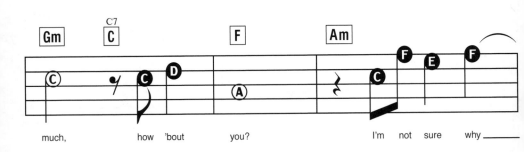

much, how 'bout you? I'm not sure why _____

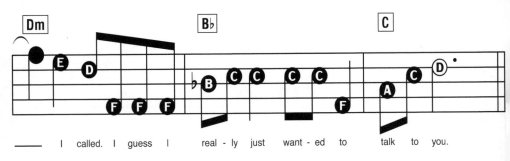

_____ I called. I guess I real - ly just want - ed to talk to you.

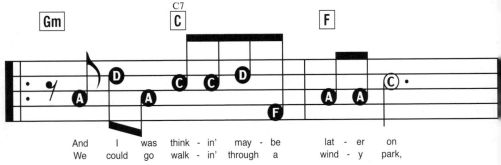

And I was think - in' may - be lat - er on
We could go walk - in' through a wind - y park,

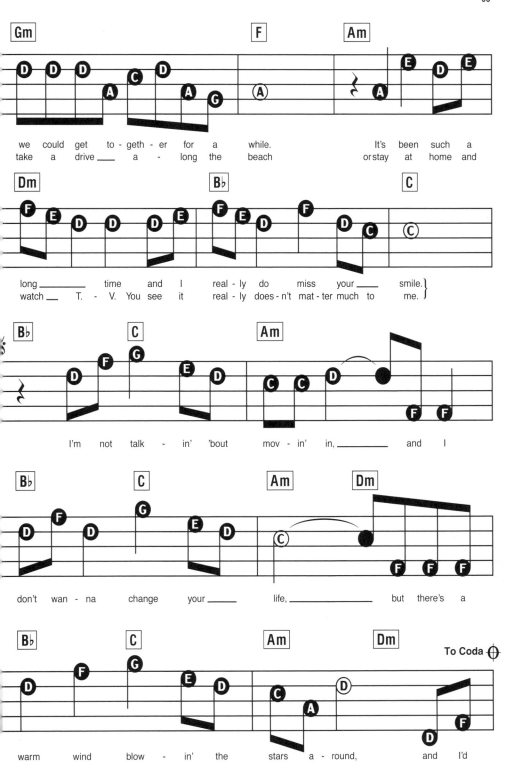

100

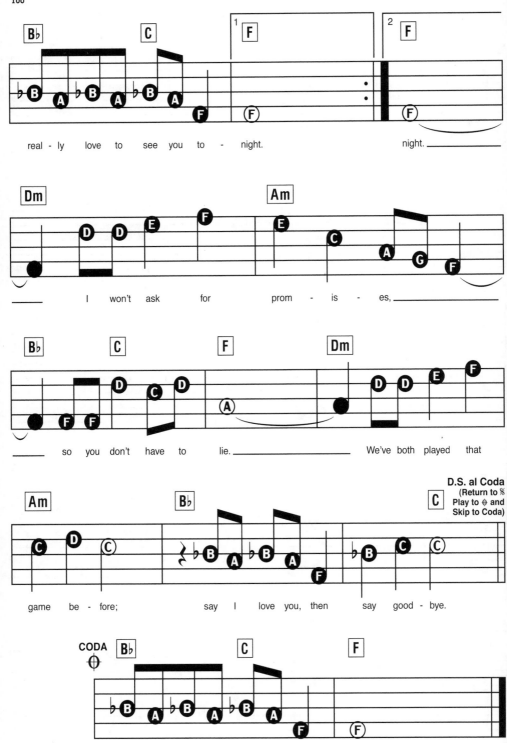

If You Don't Know Me by Now

Registration 1
Rhythm: Waltz

Words and Music by Kenneth Gamble
and Leon Huff

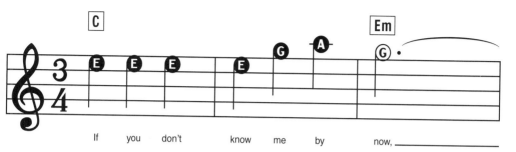

If you don't know me by now, _____

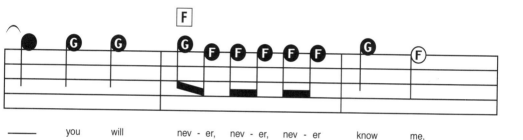

_____ you will nev- er, nev- er, nev- er know me,

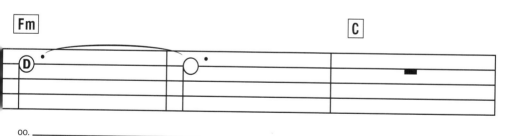

oo. _____

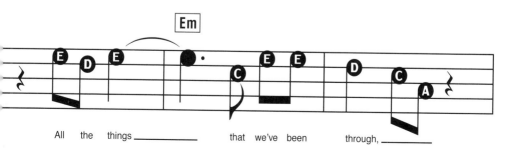

All the things _____ that we've been through, _____

102

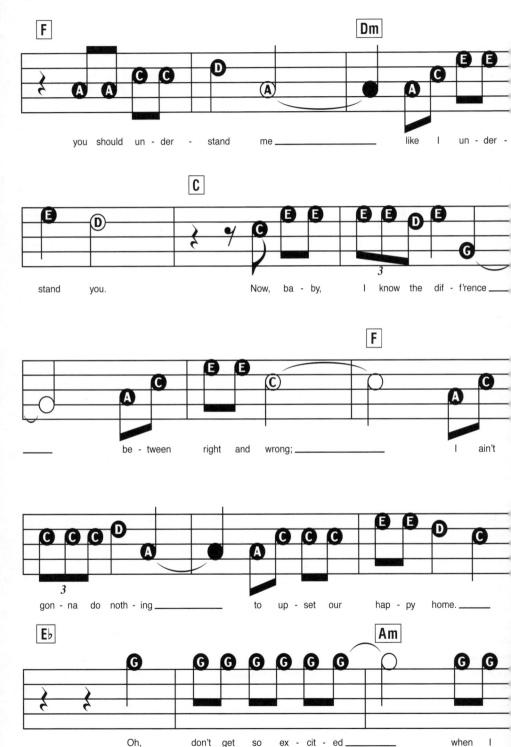

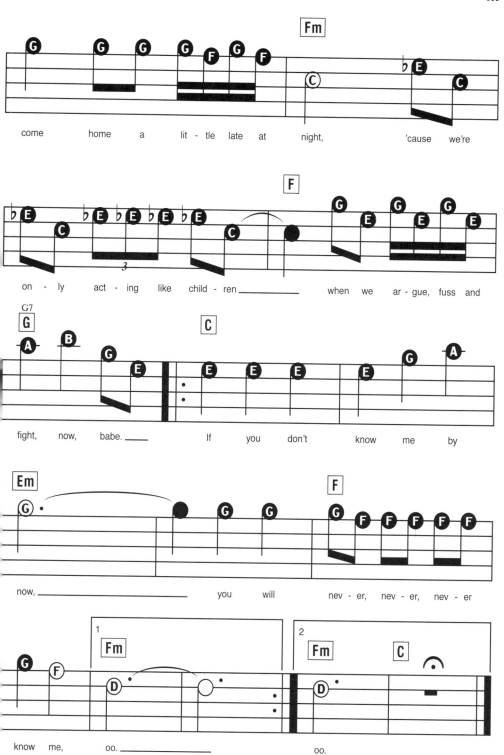

I'll Never Fall in Love Again

from PROMISES, PROMISES

Registration 1
Rhythm: Pops or Rock

Lyric by Hal David
Music by Burt Bacharach

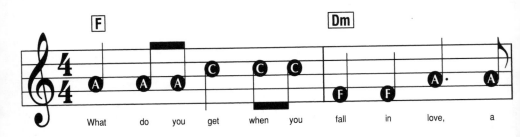

What do you get when you fall in love, a

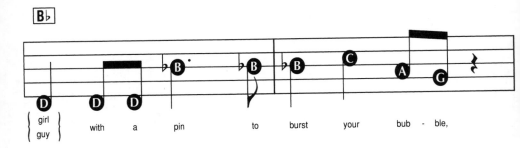

{ girl / guy } with a pin to burst your bub - ble,

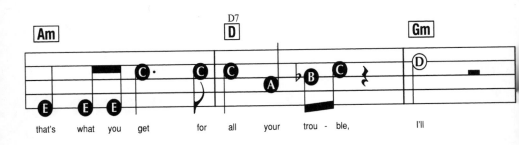

that's what you get for all your trou - ble, I'll

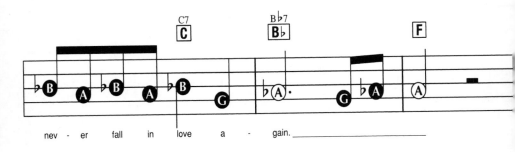

nev - er fall in love a - gain. _____

105

106

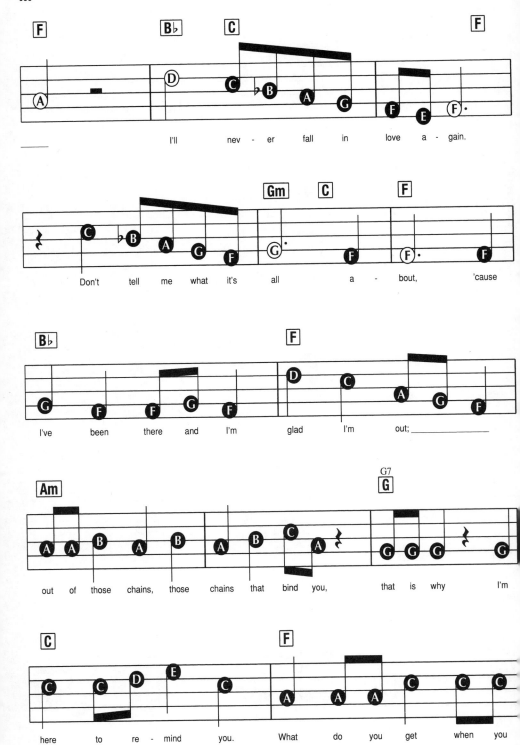

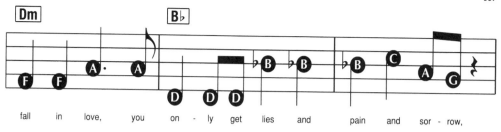

fall in love, you on - ly get lies and pain and sor - row,

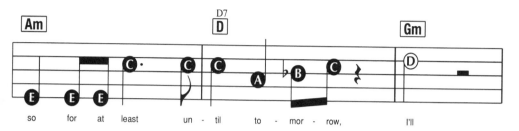

so for at least un - til to - mor - row, I'll

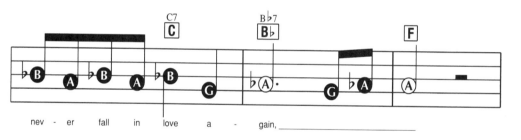

nev - er fall in love a - gain, _____

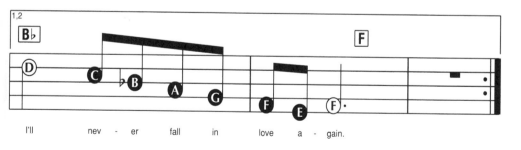

I'll nev - er fall in love a - gain.

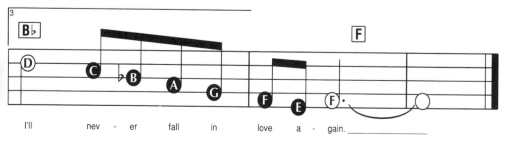

I'll nev - er fall in love a - gain. _____

If

Registration 2
Rhythm: Slow Rock or Ballad

Words and Music by
David Gates

If a picture paints a thou-sand words then why can't I paint you?
man could be two plac-es at one time I'd be with you.

The words will nev-er show the you I've come to know.
To-mor-row and to-day be-side you all the way.

If a face could launch a thou-sand ships, then where am I to go?
If the world should stop re-volv-ing, spin-ning slow-ly down to die,

There's no one home, but you, you're all that's left me to.
I'd spend the end with you and when the world was through

And when, my love for life is run-ning

109

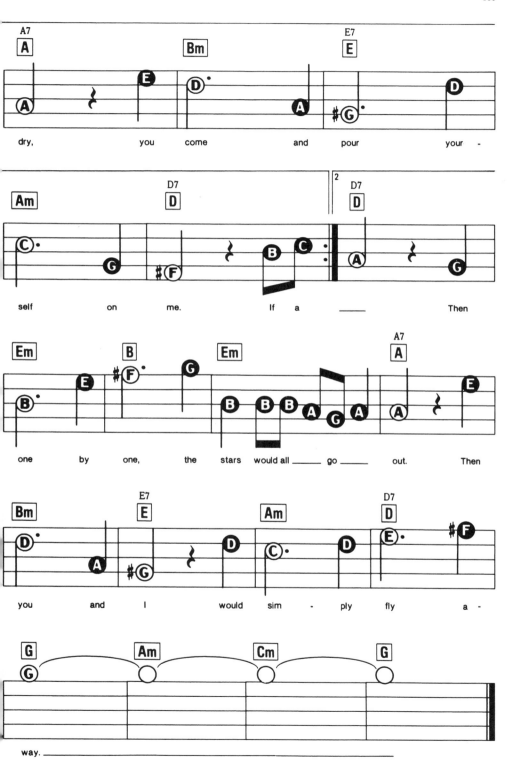

Imagine

Registration 8
Rhythm: 8-Beat or Rock

Words and Music by
John Lennon

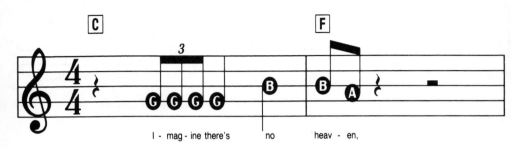

I - mag - ine there's no heav - en,

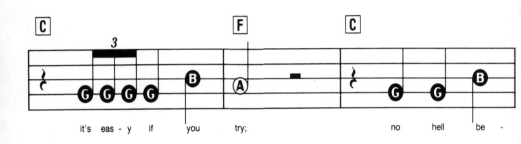

it's eas - y if you try; no hell be -

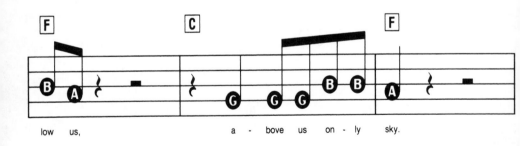

low us, a - bove us on - ly sky.

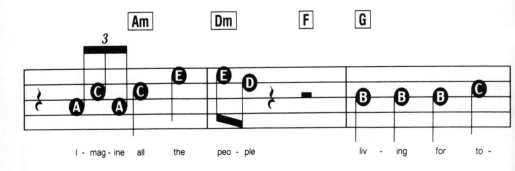

I - mag - ine all the peo - ple liv - ing for to -

111

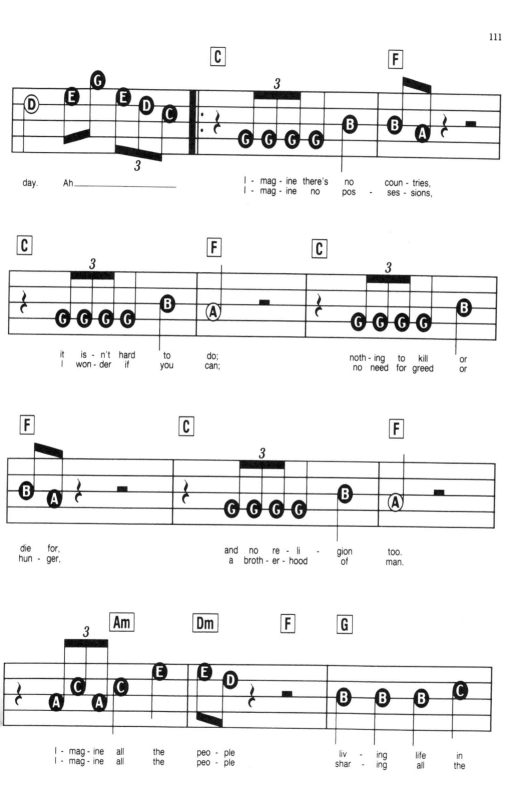

112

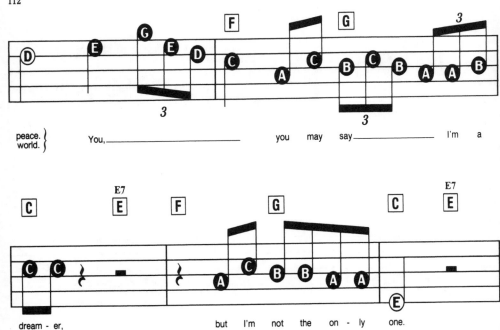

peace.
world. } You,_____ you may say_____ I'm a

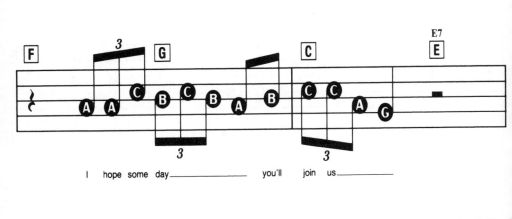

dream - er, but I'm not the on - ly one.

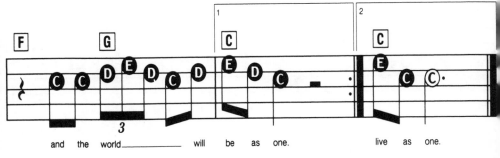

I hope some day_____ you'll join us_____

and the world_____ will be as one. live as one.

It Never Rains
in Southern California

Registration 8
Rhythm: Rock

Words and Music by Albert Hammond
and Michael Hazlewood

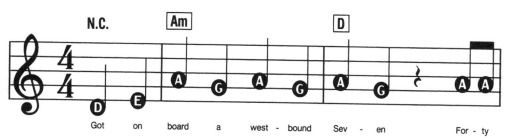

Got on board a west - bound Sev - en For - ty

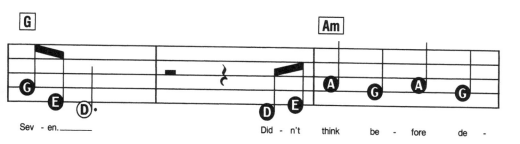

Sev - en._____ Did - n't think be - fore de -

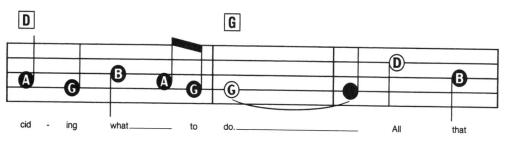

cid - ing what_____ to do._____ All that

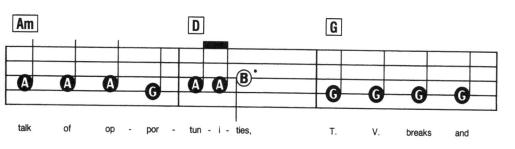

talk of op - por - tun - i - ties, T. V. breaks and

114

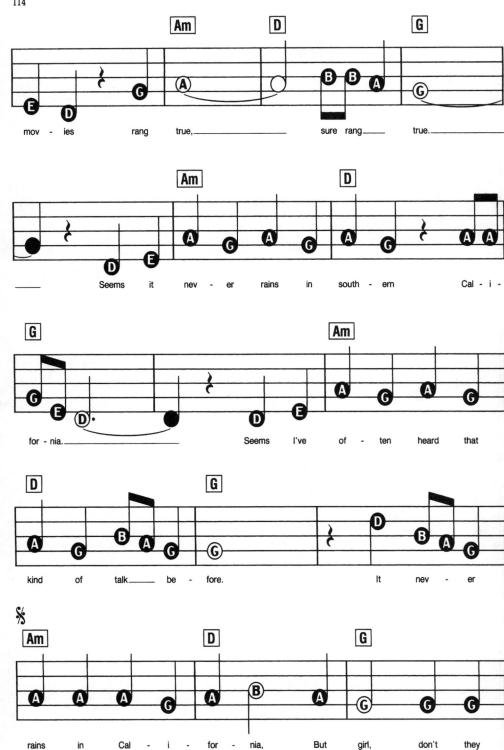

115

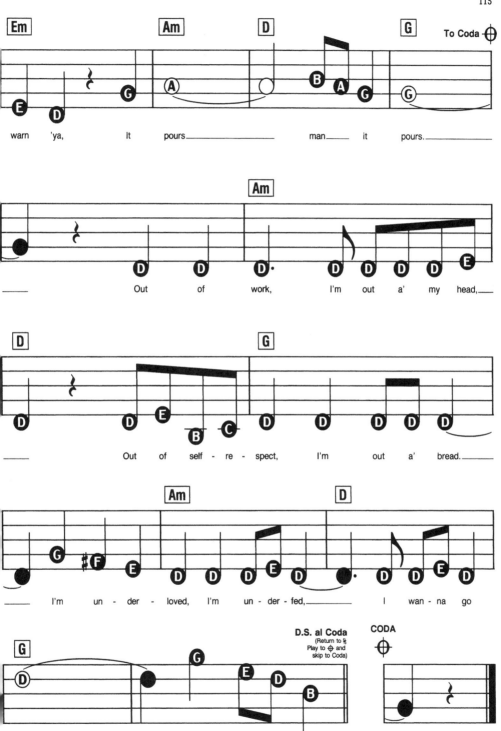

It Was a Very Good Year

Registration 9
Rhythm: Pops or Rock

Words and Music by
Ervin Drake

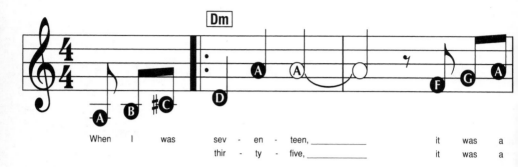

When I was sev - en - teen, _____ it was a
thir - ty - five, _____ it was a

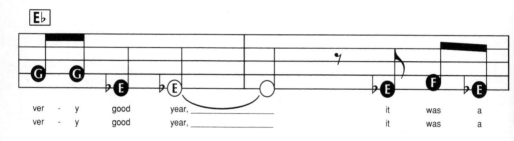

ver - y good year, _____ it was a
ver - y good year, _____ it was a

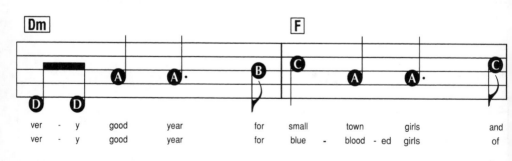

ver - y good year for small town girls and
ver - y good year for blue - blood - ed girls of

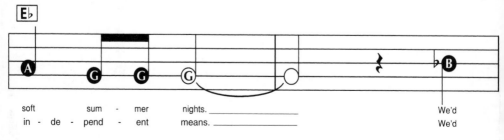

soft sum - mer nights. _____ We'd
in - de - pend - ent means. _____ We'd

117

118

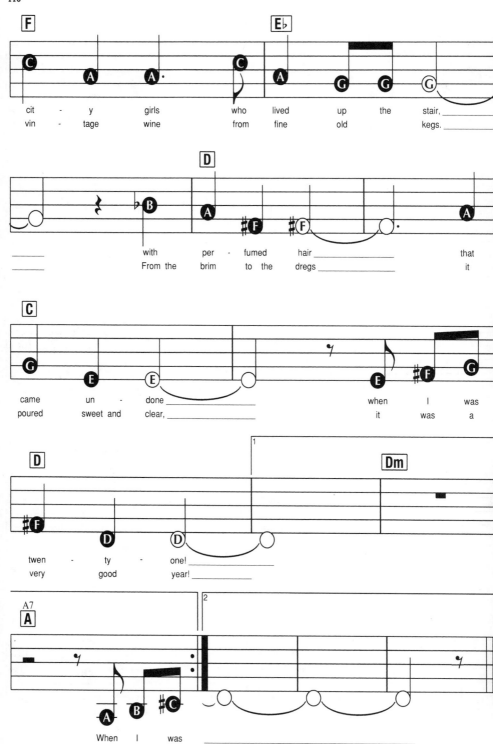

Just Once

Registration 8
Rhythm: Ballad or Slow Rock

Words by Cynthia Weil
Music by Barry Mann

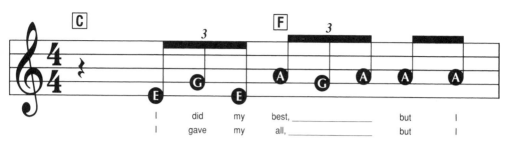

I did my best, _____ but I
I gave my all, _____ but I

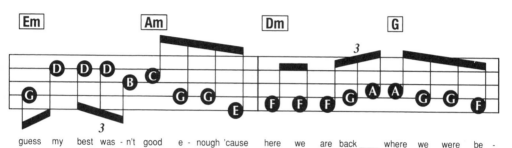

guess my best was - n't good e - nough 'cause here we are back _____ where we were be -
think my all may have been too much 'cause Lord knows, we're not _____ get - ting an - y -

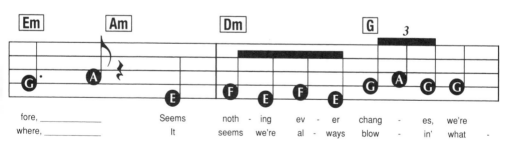

fore, _____ Seems noth - ing ev - er chang - es, we're
where, _____ It seems we're al - ways blow - in' what -

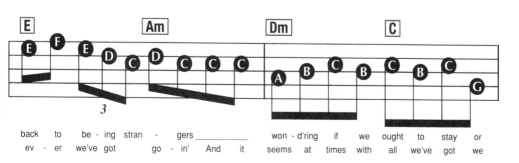

back to be - ing stran - gers _____ won - d'ring if we ought to stay or
ev - er we've got go - in' And it seems at times with all we've got we

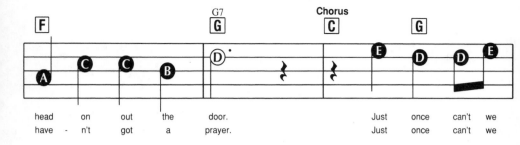

head on out the door. Just once can't we
have - n't got a prayer. Just once can't we

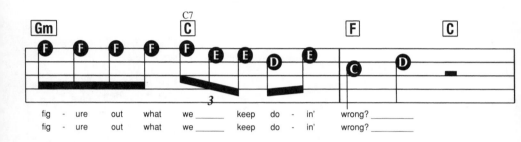

fig - ure out what we _____ keep do - in' wrong? _____
fig - ure out what we _____ keep do - in' wrong? _____

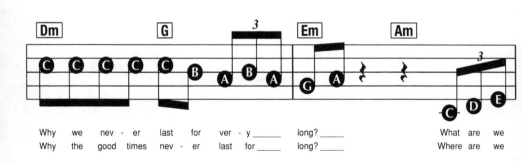

Why we nev - er last for ver - y _____ long? _____ What are we
Why the good times nev - er last for _____ long? _____ Where are we

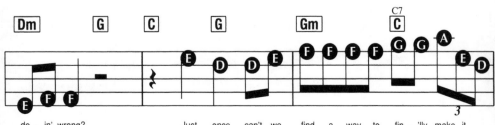

do - in' wrong? Just once can't we find a way to fin - 'lly make it _____
go - in' wrong? Just once can't we find a way to fin - 'lly make it _____

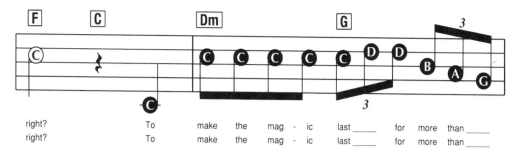

right? To make the mag - ic last _____ for more than _____
right? To make the mag - ic last _____ for more than _____

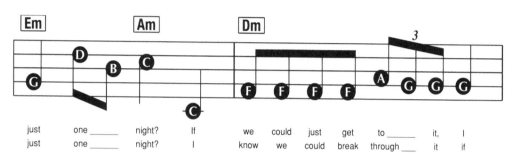

just one _____ night? If we could just get to _____ it, I
just one _____ night? I know we could break through ___ it if

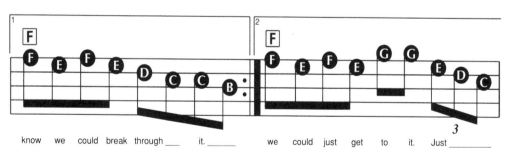

know we could break through ___ it. _____ we could just get to it. Just _____

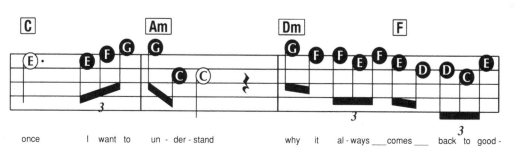

once I want to un - der - stand why it al - ways ___ comes ___ back to good-

122

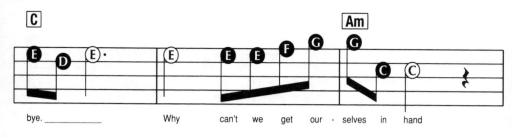

bye. _____ Why can't we get our - selves in hand

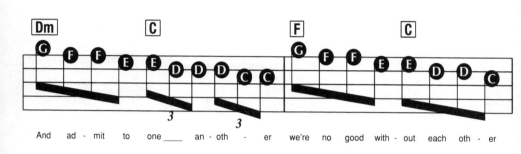

And ad - mit to one ___ an - oth - er we're no good with - out each oth - er

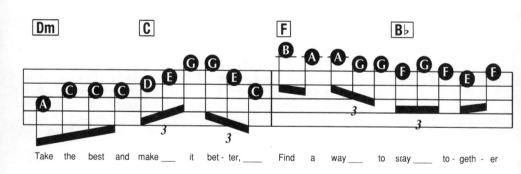

Take the best and make ___ it bet - ter, ___ Find a way ___ to stay ___ to - geth - er

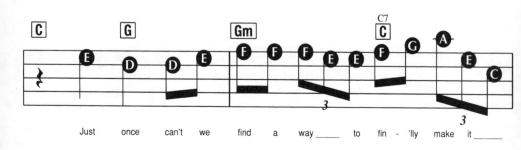

Just once can't we find a way ____ to fin - 'lly make it _____

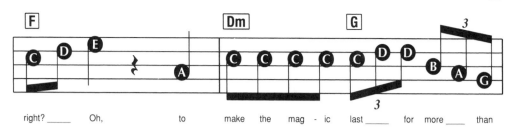

right? _____ Oh, to make the mag - ic last _____ for more _____ than

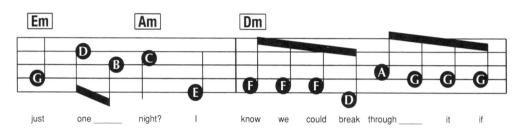

just one _____ night? I know we could break through _____ it if

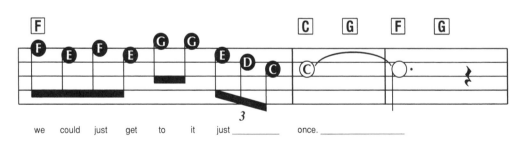

we could just get to it just _____ once. _____

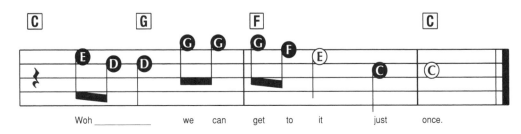

Woh _____ we can get to it just once.

124

Lady

Registration 1
Rhythm: Rock

Words and Music by
Graham Goble

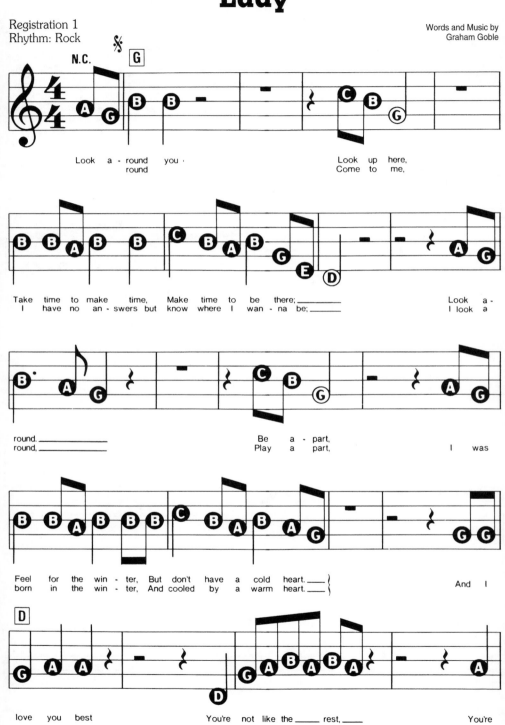

Look a - round you
round

Look up here,
Come to me,

Take time to make time, Make time to be there; _____
I have no an - swers but know where I wan - na be; _____

Look a -
I look a -

round. _____
round, _____

Be a - part,
Play a part,

I was

Feel for the win - ter, But don't have a cold heart. _____
born in the win - ter, And cooled by a warm heart. _____

And I

love you best

You're not like the _____ rest, _____

You're

© 1978 WARNER/CHAPPELL PTY. LTD.
All Rights in the U.S. and Canada Administered by WB MUSIC CORP.
All Rights Reserved   Used by Permission

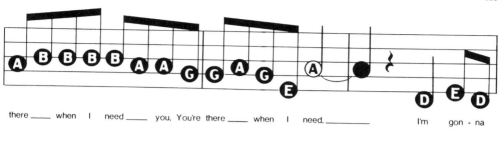

there ____ when I need ____ you, You're there ____ when I need, _____ I'm gon-na

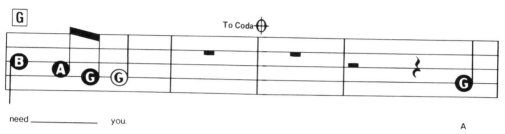

need _____ you.

A

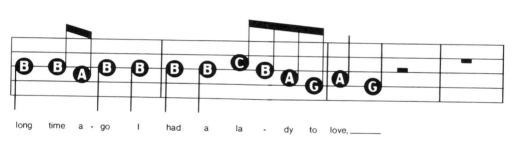

long time a - go I had a la - dy to love,_____

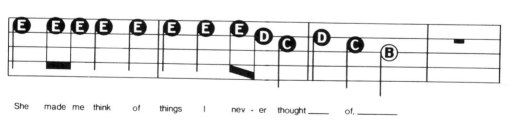

She made me think of things I nev-er thought ____ of, _____

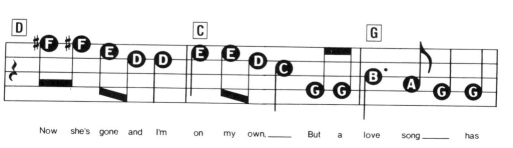

Now she's gone and I'm on my own,_____ But a love song _____ has

126

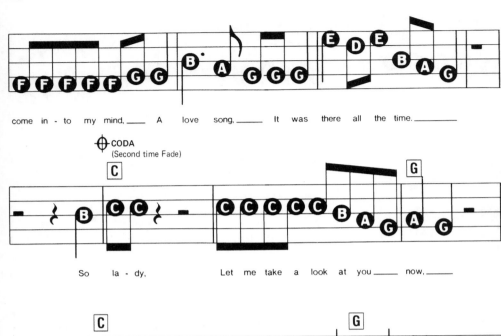

come in - to my mind, ___ A love song, ___ It was there all the time. _____

(Second time Fade)

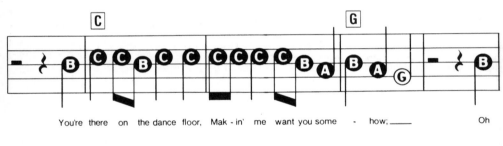

So la - dy, Let me take a look at you ___ now, ___

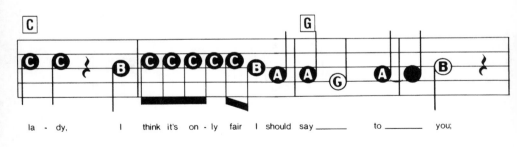

You're there on the dance floor, Mak - in' me want you some - how; ___ Oh

lady, I think it's on - ly fair I should say ___ to ___ you;

D.S. al Coda
and Fade

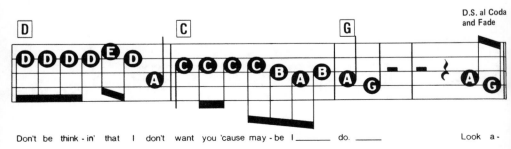

Don't be think - in' that I don't want you 'cause may - be I ___ do. ___ Look a-

Leather and Lace

Registration 2
Rhythm: Ballad

Words and Music by
Stevie Nicks

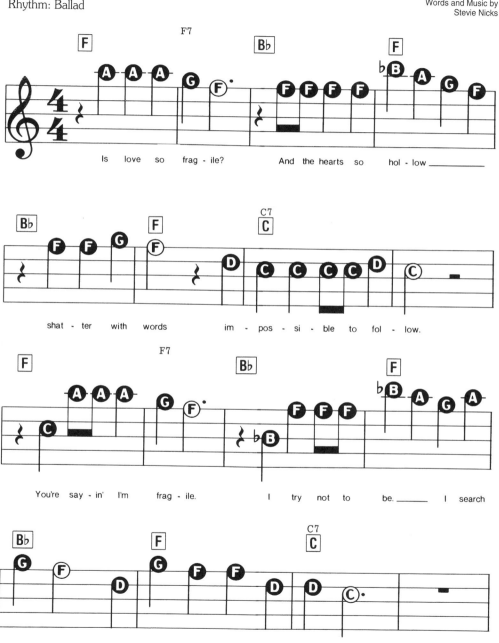

128

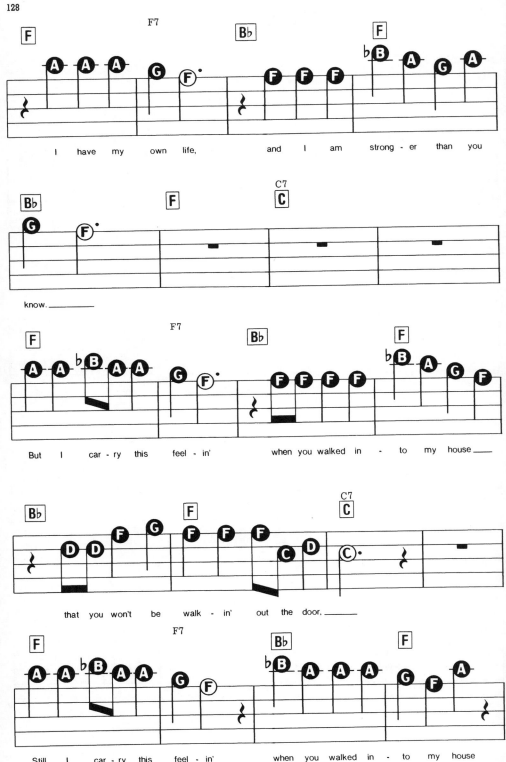

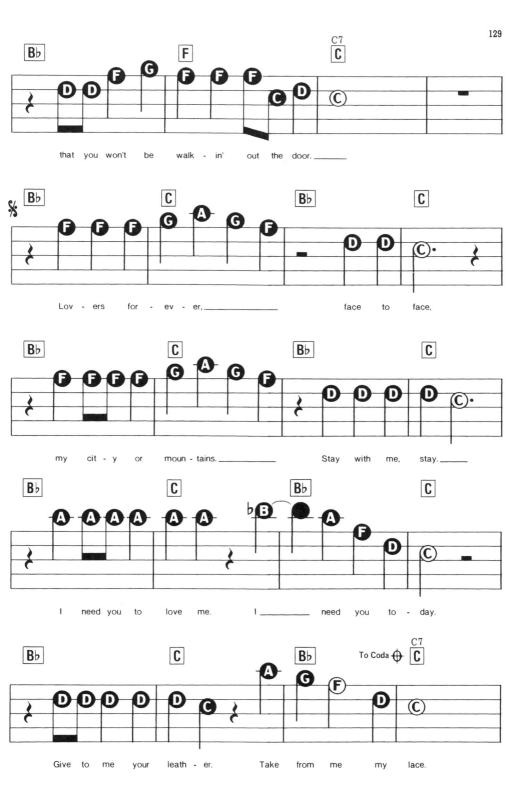

130

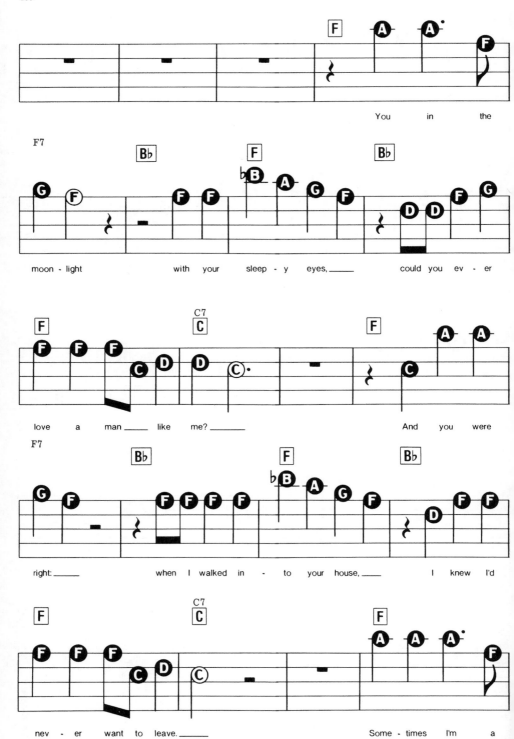

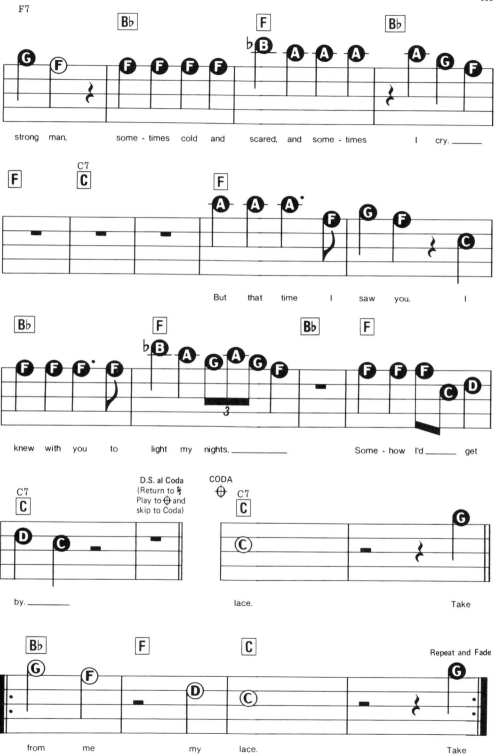

Let It Be

Registration 3
Rhythm: Rock or Pops

Words and Music by John Lennon
and Paul McCartney

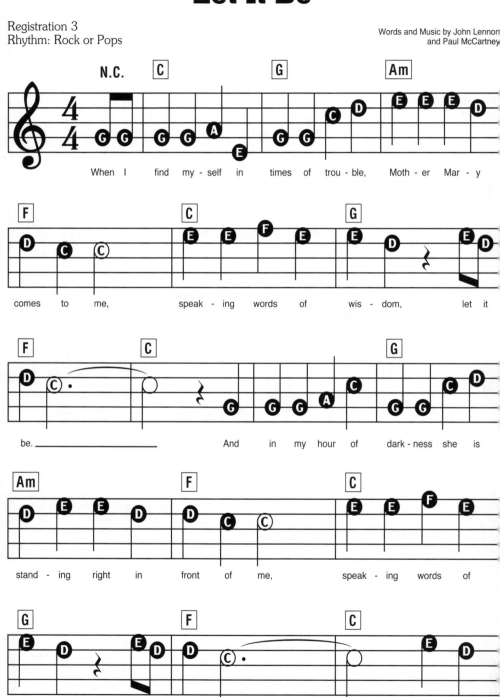

133

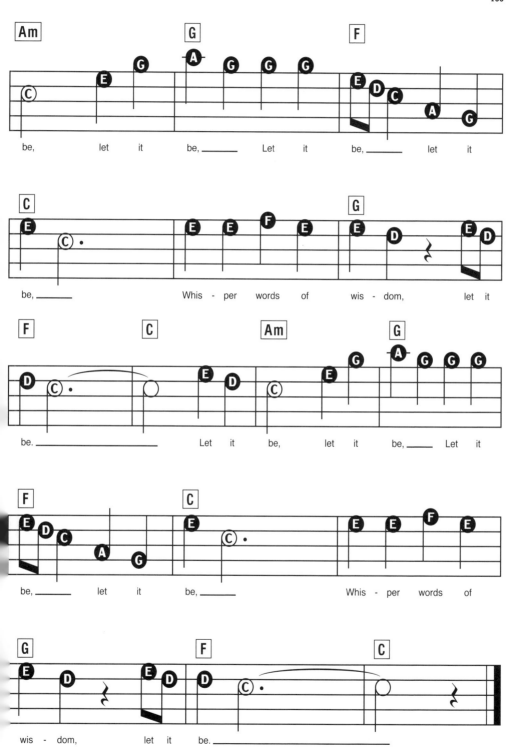

Let It Be Me
(Je t'appartiens)

Registration 8
Rhythm: Ballad

English Words by Mann Curtis
French Words by Pierre DeLanoe
Music by Gilbert Becaud

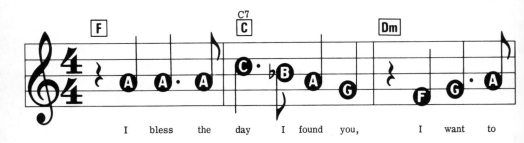

I bless the day I found you, I want to

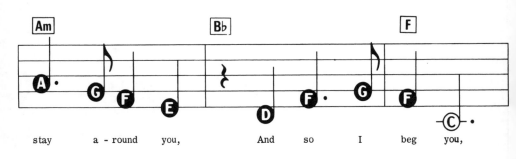

stay a - round you, And so I beg you,

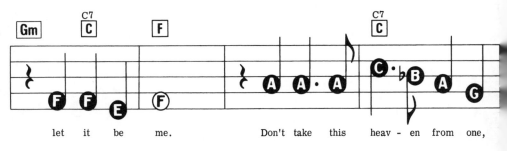

let it be me. Don't take this heav - en from one,

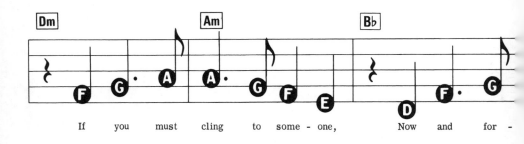

If you must cling to some - one, Now and for -

135

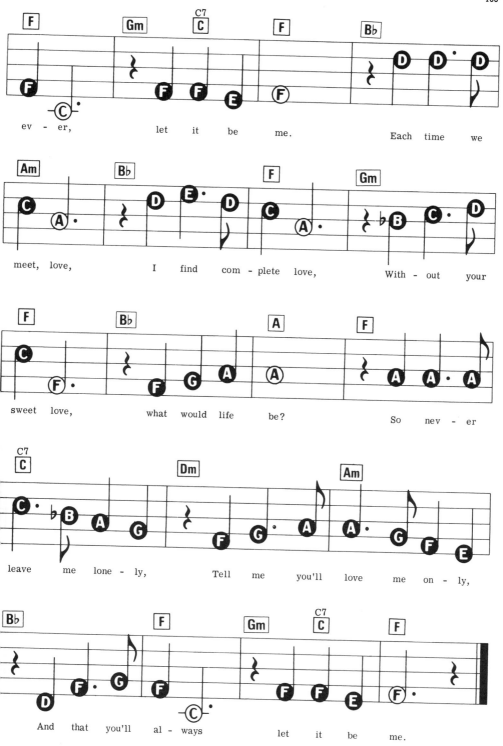

Lonely People

Registration 4
Rhythm: Folk or Rock

Words and Music by Dan Peek
and Catherine L. Peek

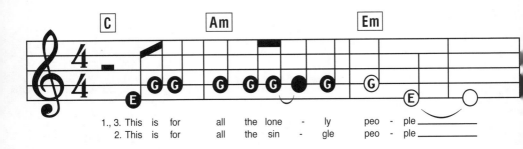

1., 3. This is for all the lone - ly peo - ple _____
2. This is for all the sin - gle peo - ple _____

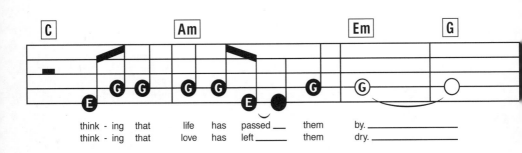

think - ing that life has passed ___ them by. _____
think - ing that love has left ____ them dry. _____

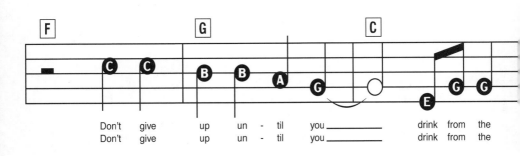

Don't give up un - til you _____ drink from the
Don't give up un - til you _____ drink from the

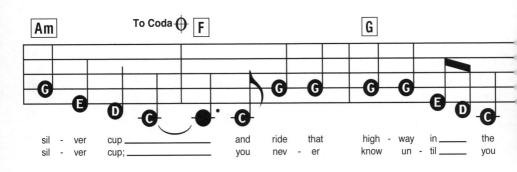

sil - ver cup _____ and ride that high - way in ___ the
sil - ver cup; _____ you nev - er know un - til ____ you

137

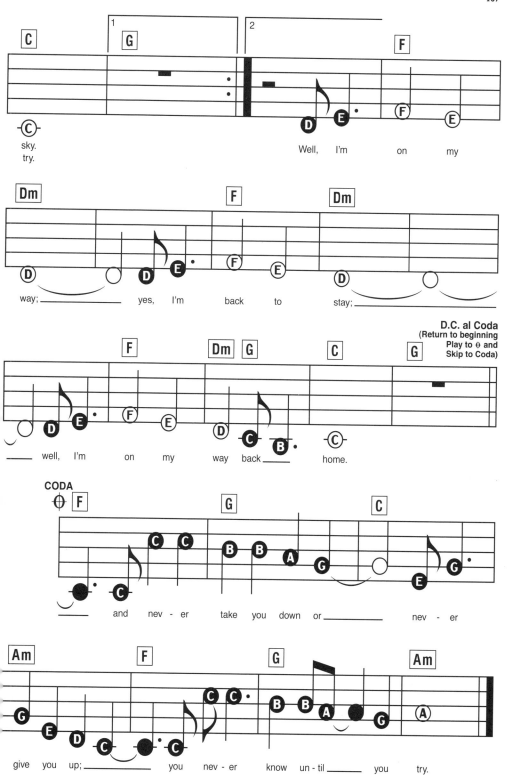

Midnight Train to Georgia

Registration 4
Rhythm: Rock

Words and Music by
Jim Weatherly

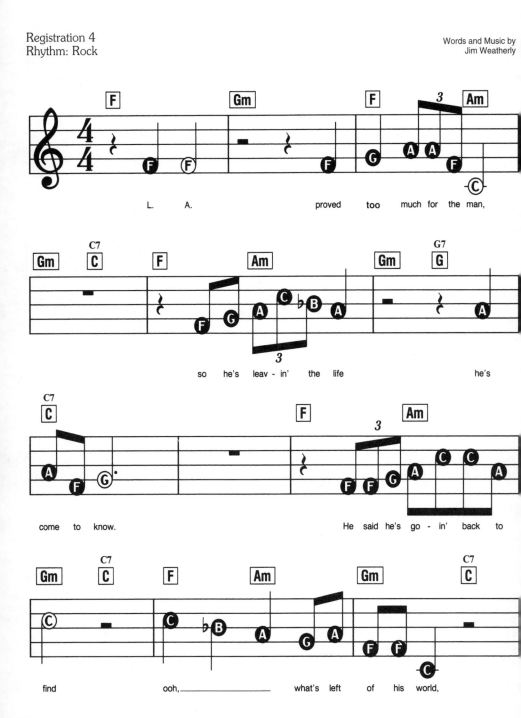

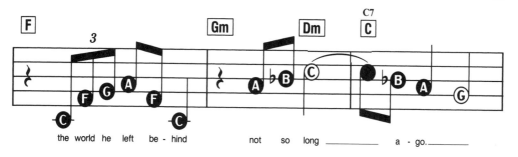

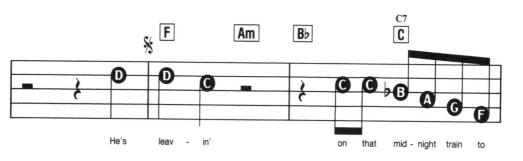

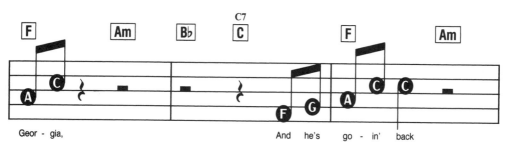

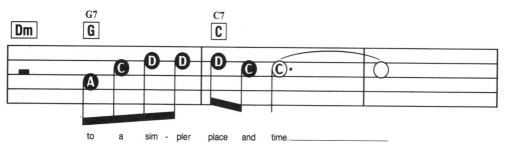

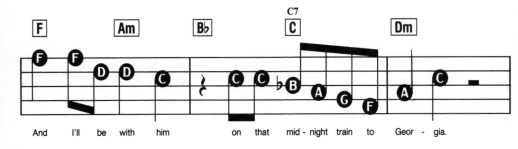

And I'll be with him on that mid - night train to Geor - gia.

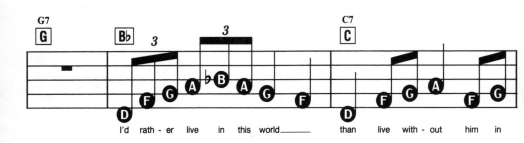

I'd rath - er live in this world___ than live with - out him in

To Coda ⊕

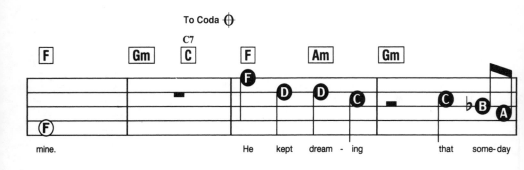

mine. He kept dream - ing that some-day

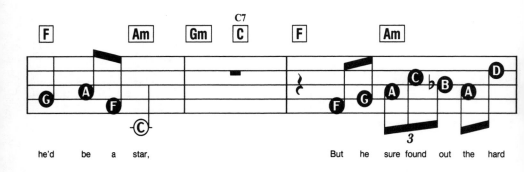

he'd be a star, But he sure found out the hard

On and On

Registration 7
Rhythm: 8-Beat or Rock

Words and Music by
Stephen Bishop

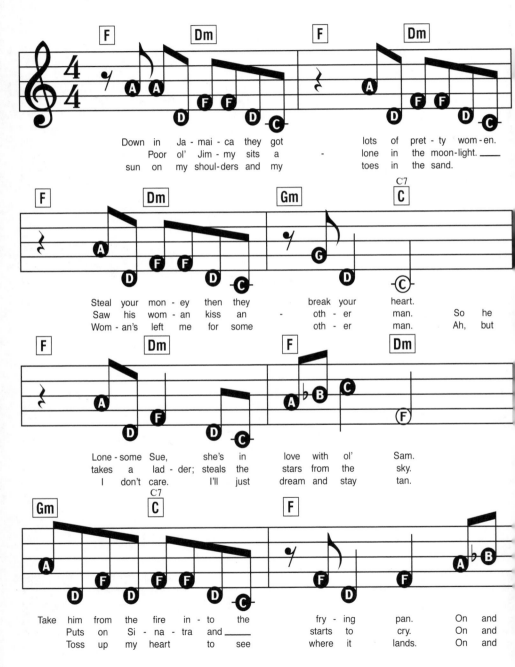

Down in Ja - mai - ca they got   lots of pret - ty wom - en.
Poor ol' Jim - my sits a -   lone in the moon - light.
sun on my shoul - ders and my   toes in the sand.

Steal your mon - ey then they   break your heart. So he
Saw his wom - an kiss an -   oth - er man. Ah, but
Wom - an's left me for some   oth - er man.

Lone - some Sue, she's in   love with ol' Sam.
takes a lad - der; steals the   stars from the sky.
I don't care. I'll just   dream and stay tan.

Take him from the fire in - to the   fry - ing pan. On and
Puts on Si - na - tra and   starts to cry. On and
Toss up my heart to see   where it lands. On and

143

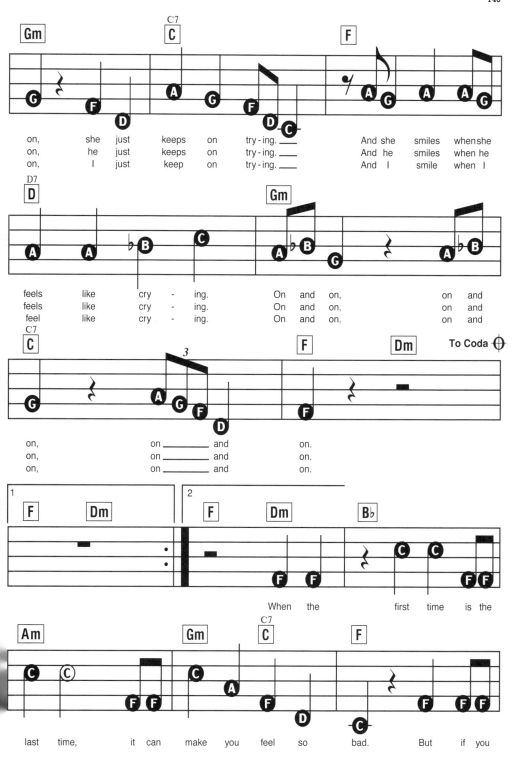

144

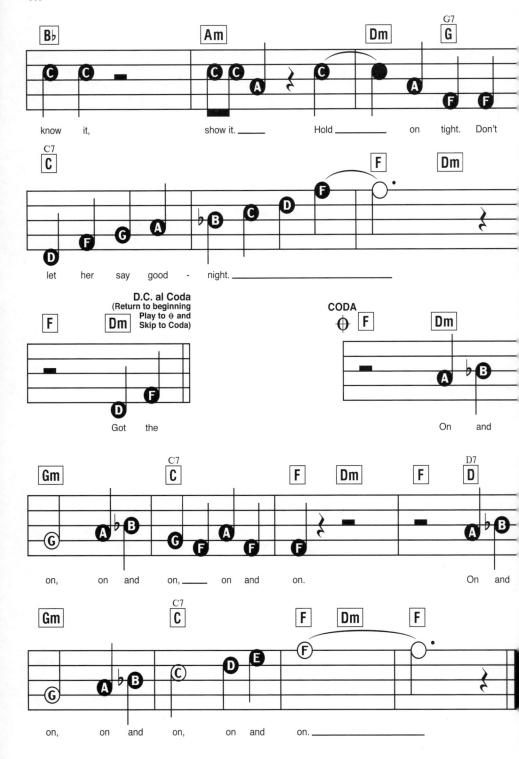

On My Own

Registration 2
Rhythm: 8-Beat or Rock

Words and Music by Carole Bayer Sager
and Burt Bacharach

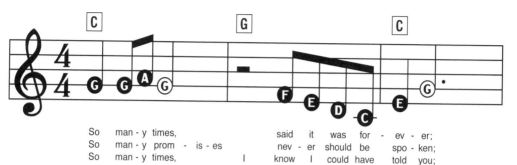

So man - y times,   said it was for - ev - er;
So man - y prom - is - es   nev - er should be spo - ken;
So man - y times,   I know I could have told you;

said our love would al - ways be true. _____
now I know what lov - ing you cost. _____
los - in' you, it cuts like a knife. _____

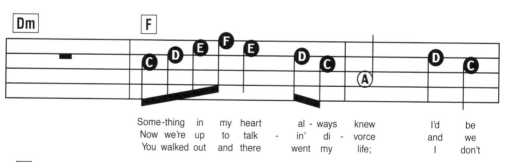

Some - thing in my heart al - ways knew I'd be
Now we're up to talk - in' di - vorce and we
You walked out and there went my life; I don't

To Coda

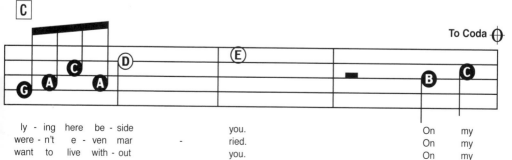

ly - ing here be - side   you.   On my
were - n't e - ven mar -   ried.   On my
want to live with - out   you.   On my

146

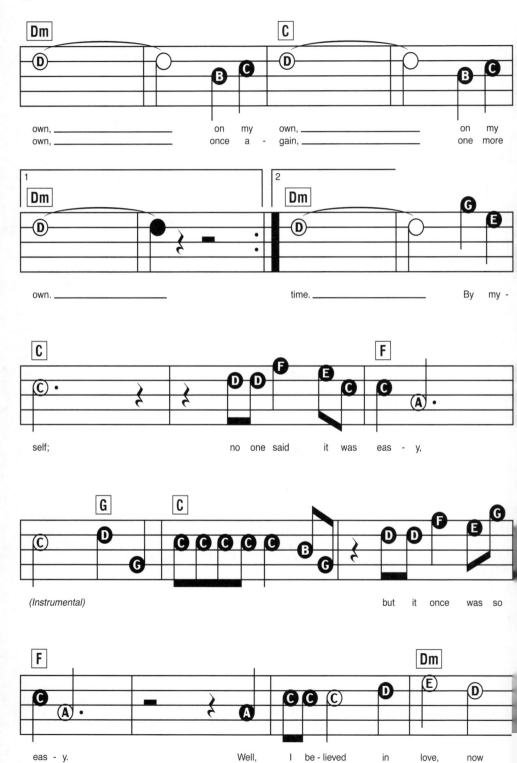

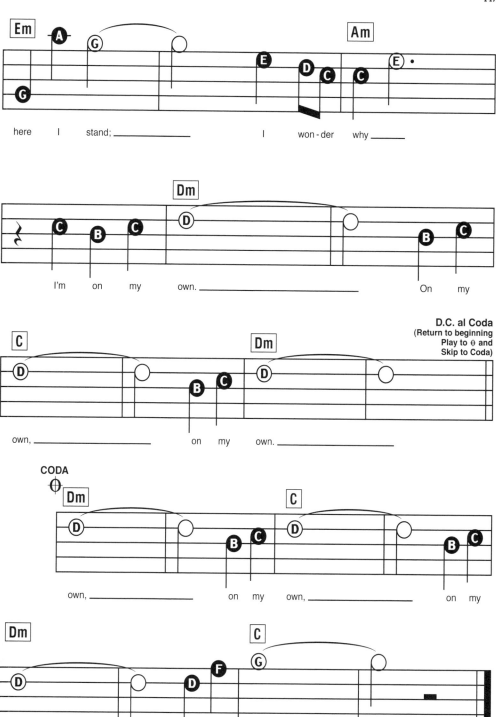

One More Night

Registration 3
Rhythm: Latin or Rock

right

Words and Music by
Phil Collins

I've been try - ing for so long_____ to
I've been sit - ting here so so long_____
I know there'll nev - er be a time_____ you'll ever

let you know,_____ how I
wast - ing time,_____ just star - ing at the
feel the same,_____ and I know it's on - ly

feel
phone
right

and if I
and I was
but if you

stum - ble, if I fall_____ just help me back,_____
won - d'ring should I call you just then I thought be here,_____
change your mind,_____ you know that I'll

150

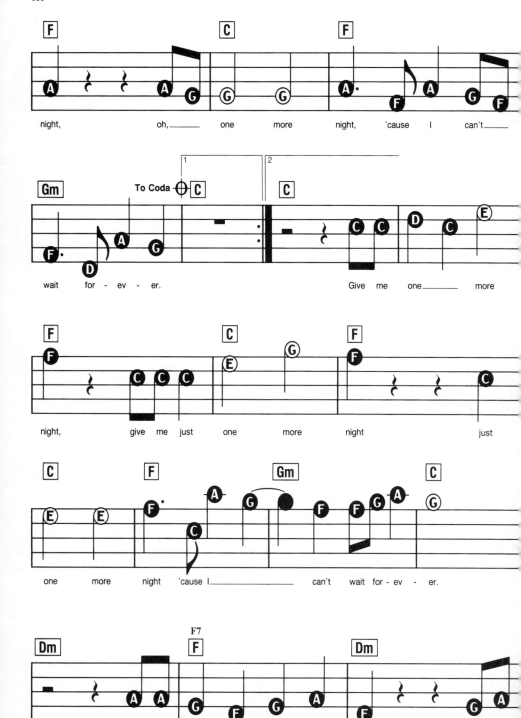

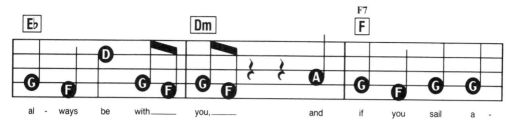

al - ways be with___ you,___ and if you sail a -

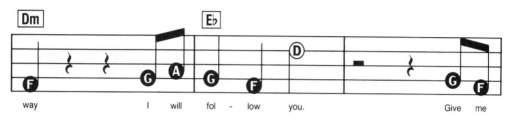

way I will fol - low you. Give me

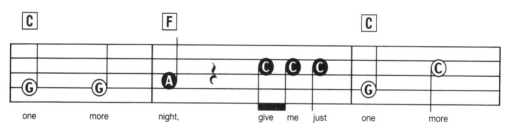

one more night, give me just one more

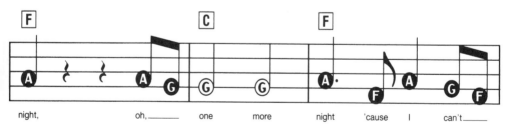

night, oh,___ one more night 'cause I can't___

D.C. al Coda
(Return to beginning
Play to ⊕ and
skip to Coda)

CODA
⊕ C

D.S. and Fade
(Return to 𝄋
and Fade)

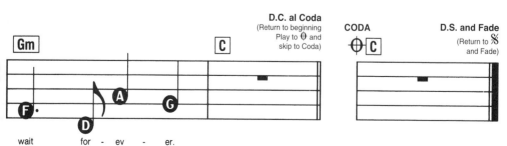

wait for - ev - er.

Our House

Registration 1
Rhythm: Ballad or Soft Rock

Words and Music by
Graham Nash

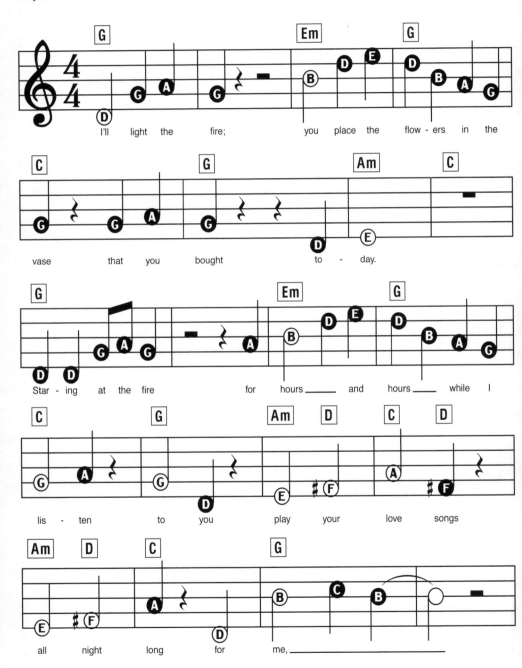

153

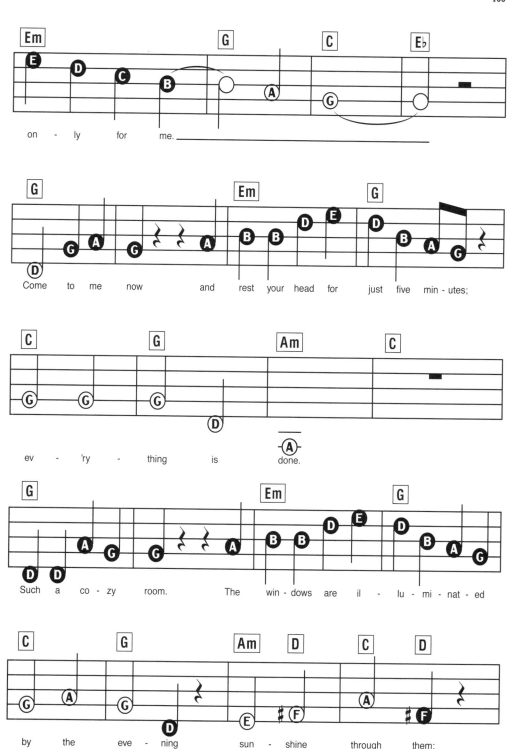

154

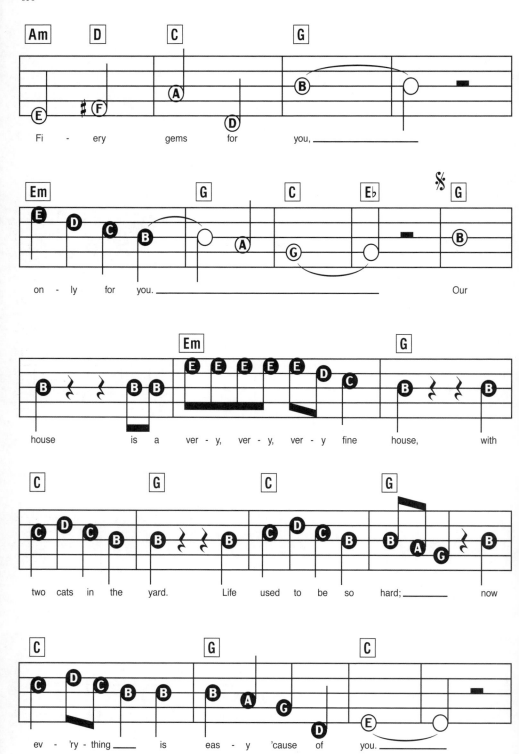

155

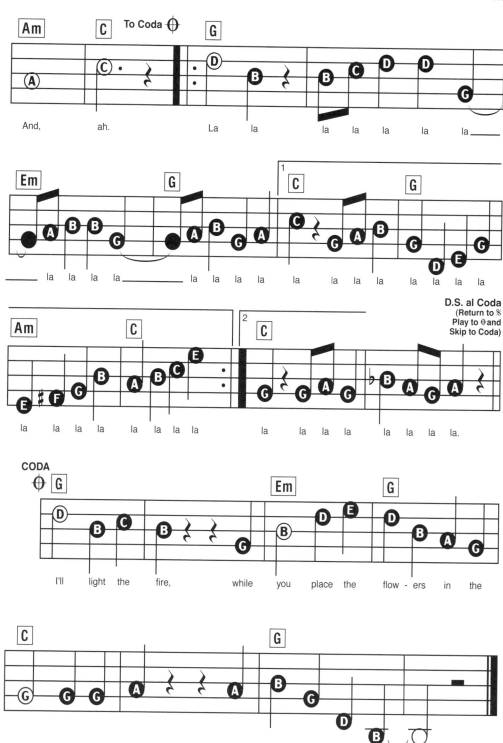

Over the Rainbow
from THE WIZARD OF OZ

Registration 5
Rhythm: Fox Trot

Music by Harold Arlen
Lyric by E.Y. "Yip" Harburg

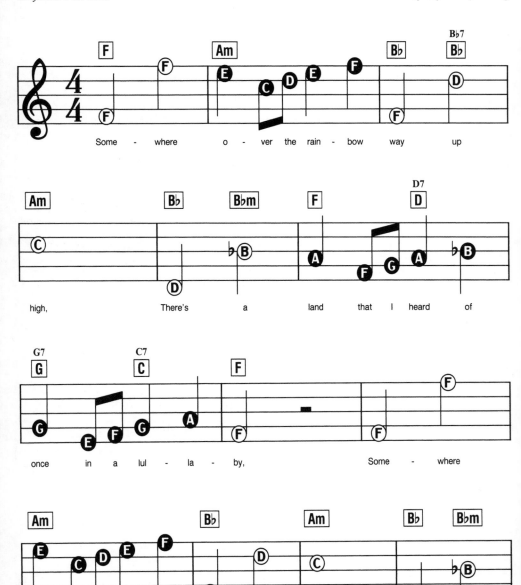

157

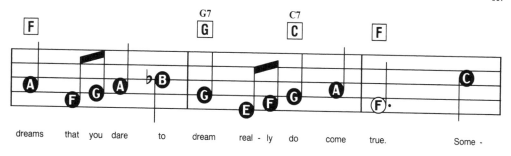

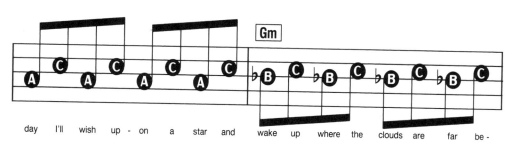

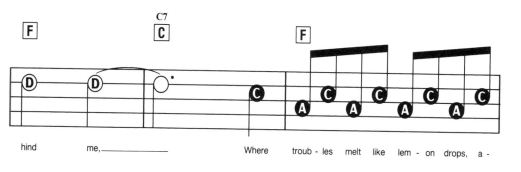

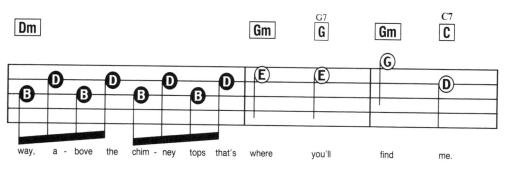

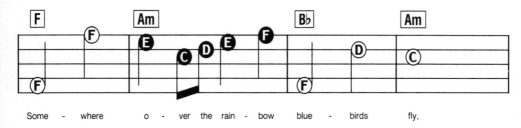

Some - where   o - ver the rain - bow   blue - birds   fly,

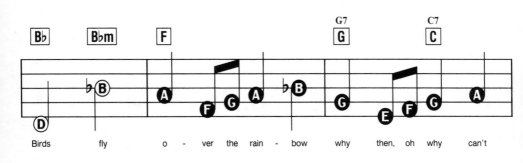

Birds   fly   o - ver the rain - bow   why   then, oh   why   can't

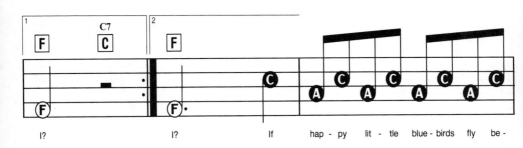

I?   I?   If   hap - py   lit - tle   blue - birds   fly   be -

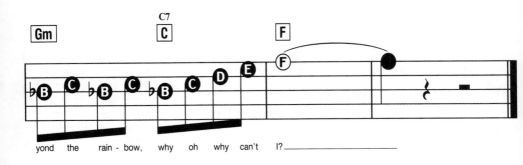

yond   the   rain - bow,   why   oh   why   can't   I?_____

The Rainbow Connection
from THE MUPPET MOVIE

Registration 4
Rhythm: Waltz

Words and Music by Paul Williams
and Kenneth L. Ascher

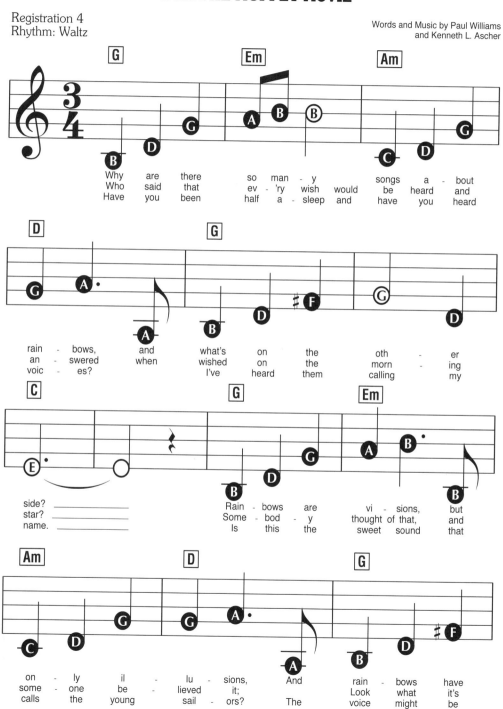

160

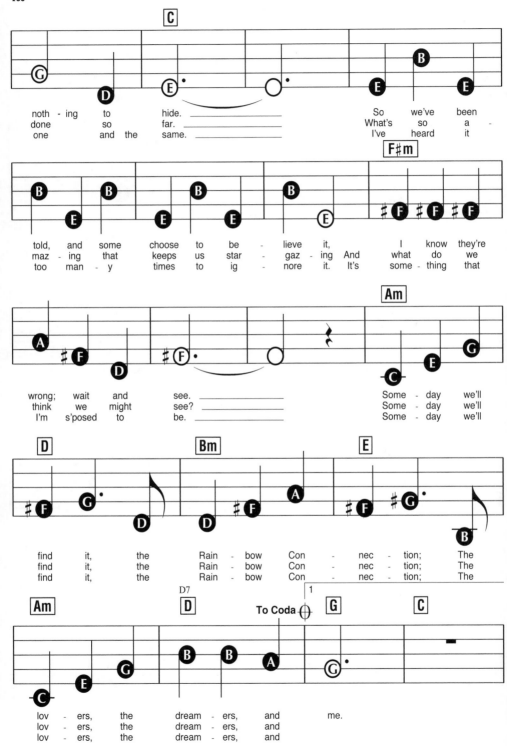

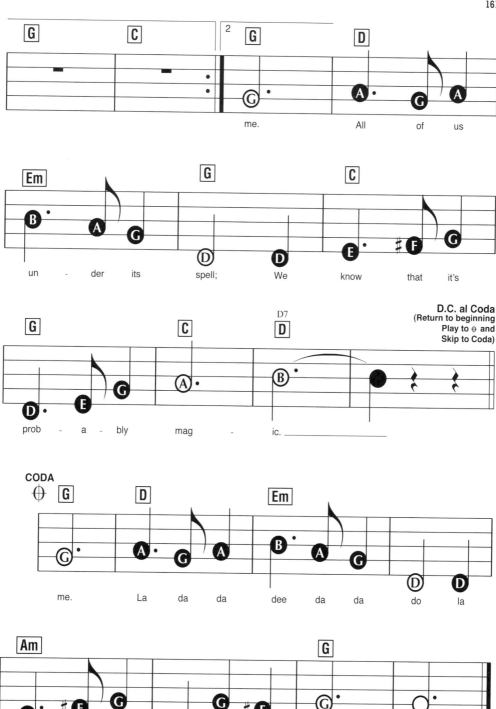

Reminiscing

Registration 4
Rhythm: Rock

Words and Music by
Graham Goble

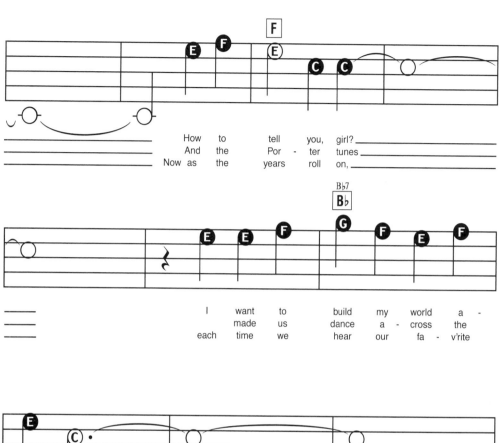

How   to   tell   you,   girl? _____
And   the   Por - ter   tunes _____
Now as   the   years   roll   on, _____

I   want   to   build   my   world   a -
made   us   dance   a - cross   the
each   time   we   hear   our   fa - v'rite

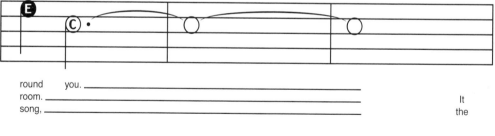

round   you. _____
room. _____
song, _____ It
the

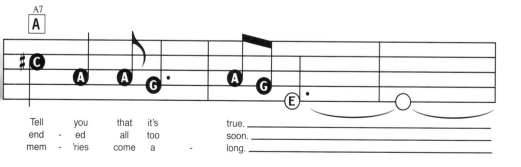

Tell   you   that   it's   true. _____
end - ed   all   too   soon. _____
mem - 'ries   come   a - long. _____

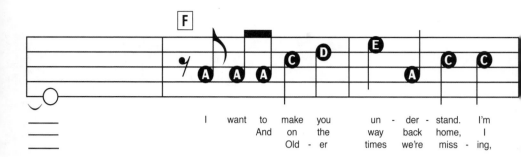

I want to make you un - der - stand. I'm
And on the way back home, I
Old - er times we're miss - ing,

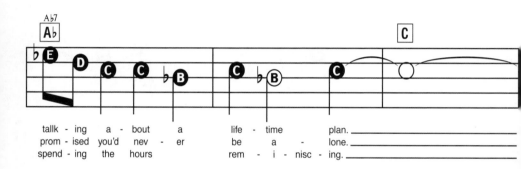

tallk - ing a - bout a life - time plan. _____
prom - ised you'd nev - er be a - lone. _____
spend - ing the hours rem - i - nisc - ing. _____

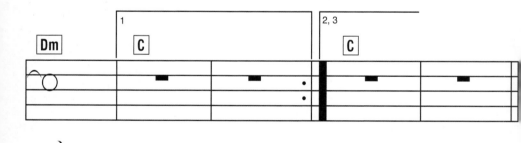

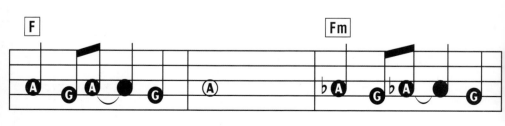

Hur - ry; don't _____ be late. I can hard - ly

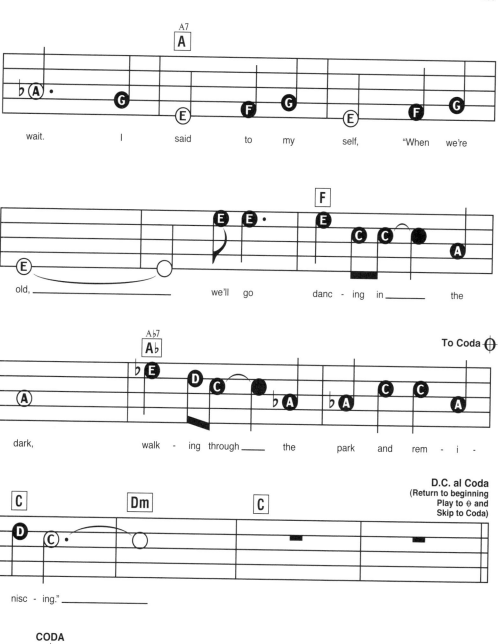

wait.   I   said   to   my   self,   "When   we're

old, _____ we'll   go   danc - ing   in _____ the

To Coda ⊕

dark,   walk - ing   through _____ the   park   and   rem - i -

D.C. al Coda
(Return to beginning
Play to ⊕ and
Skip to Coda)

nisc - ing." _____

CODA
⊕

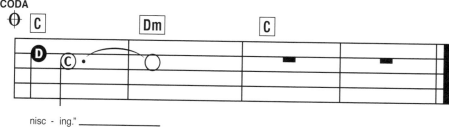

nisc - ing." _____

Right Here Waiting

Registration 8
Rhythm: 8-Beat or Rock

Words and Music by
Richard Marx

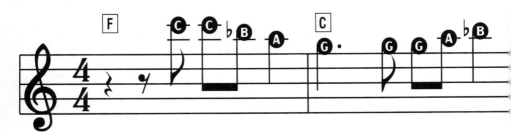

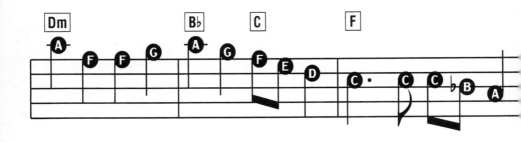

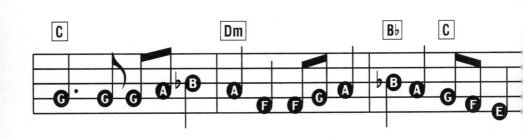

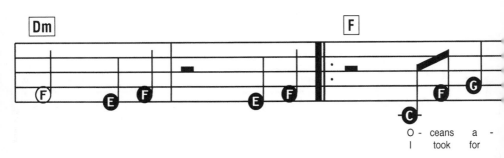

O - ceans a -
I   took for

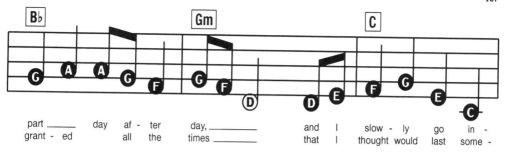

part _____ day af - ter day, _____ and I slow - ly go in -
grant - ed all the times _____ that I thought would last some -

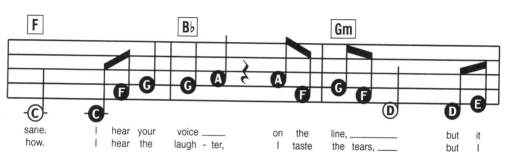

sane. I hear your voice _____ on the line, _____ but it
how. I hear the laugh - ter, I taste the tears, _____ but I

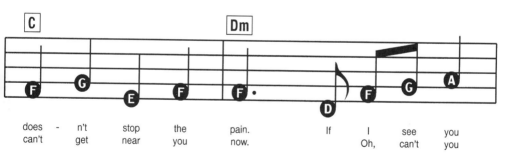

does - n't stop the pain. If I see you
can't get near you now. Oh, can't you

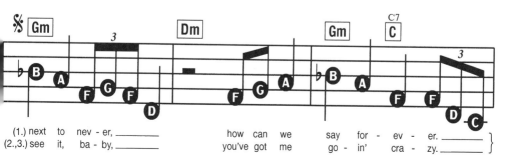

(1.) next to nev - er, _____ how can we say for - ev - er. _____
(2.,3.) see it, ba - by, _____ you've got me go - in' cra - zy. _____

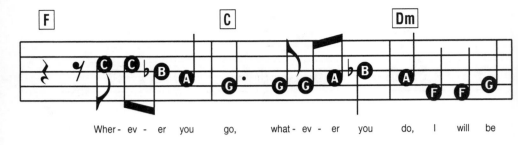

Wher - ev - er you go, what - ev - er you do, I will be

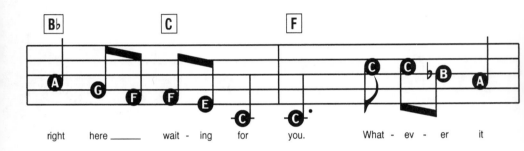

right here ____ wait - ing for you. What - ev - er it

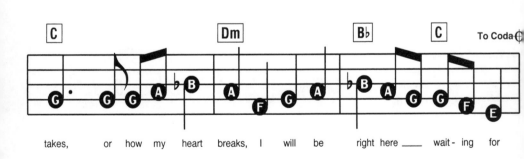

takes, or how my heart breaks, I will be right here ____ wait - ing for

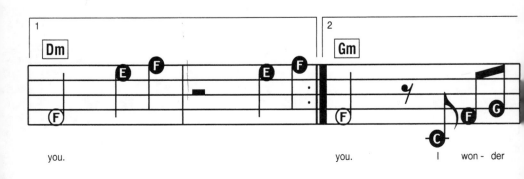

you. you. I won - der

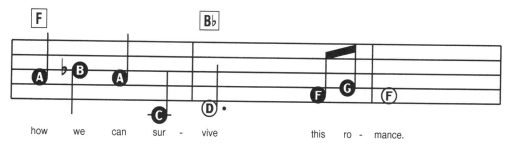

how we can sur - vive this ro - mance.

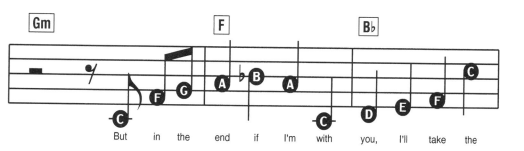

But in the end if I'm with you, I'll take the

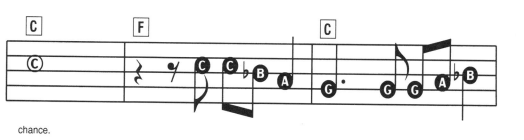

chance.

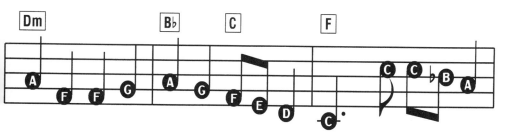

170

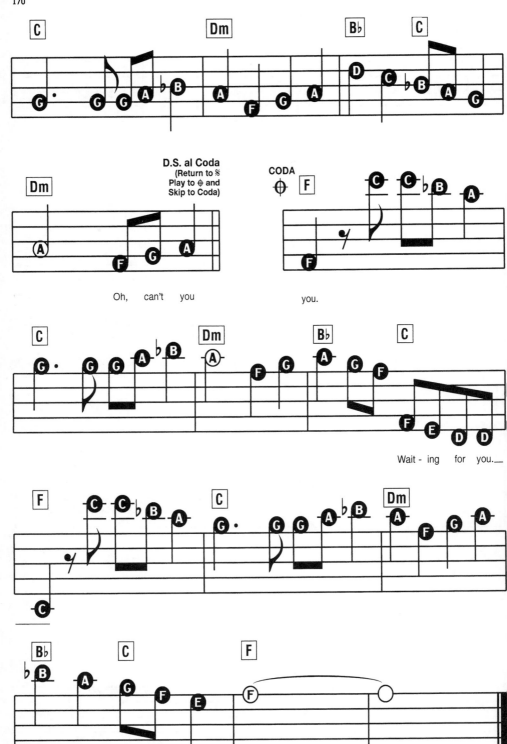

D.S. al Coda
(Return to %
Play to ⊕ and
Skip to Coda)

CODA

Oh, can't you   you.

Wait - ing   for   you.___

Sailing

Registration 2
Rhythm: Pops or 8-Beat

Words and Music by
Christopher Cross

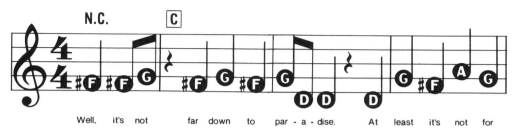

Well, it's not far down to par - a - dise. At least it's not for

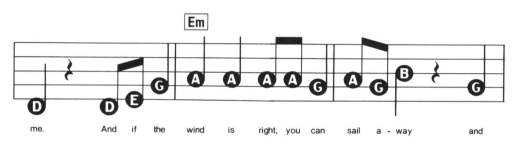

me. And if the wind is right, you can sail a - way and

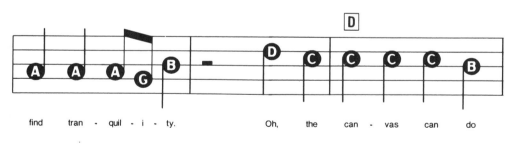

find tran - quil - i - ty. Oh, the can - vas can do

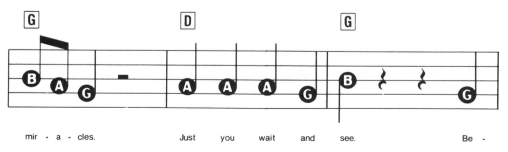

mir - a - cles. Just you wait and see. Be -

172

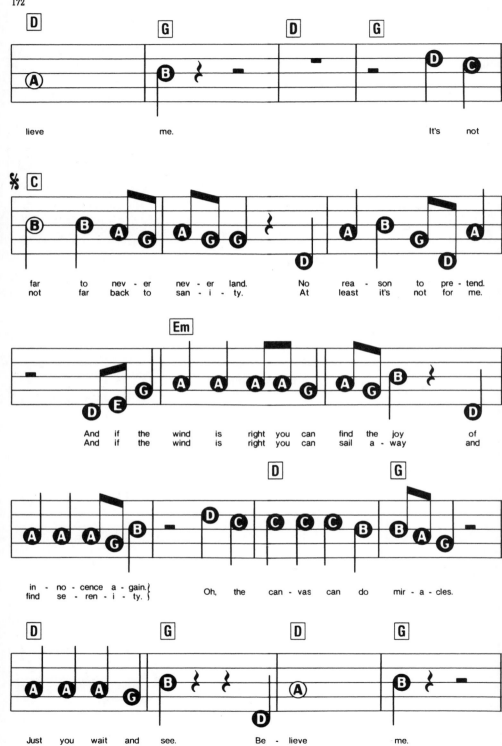

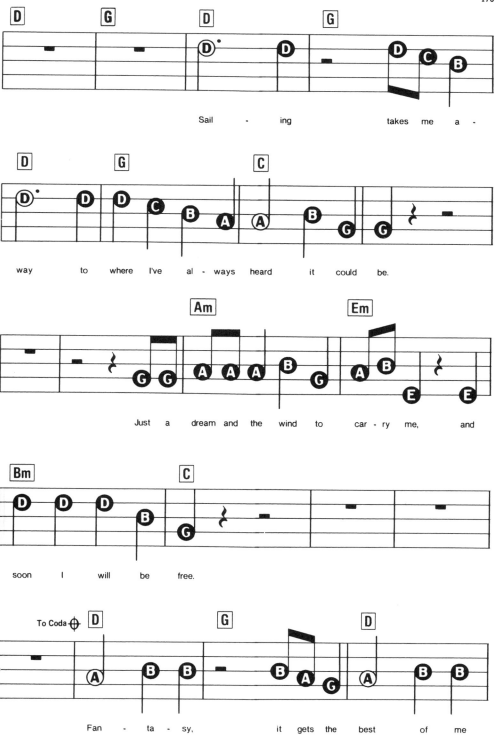

174

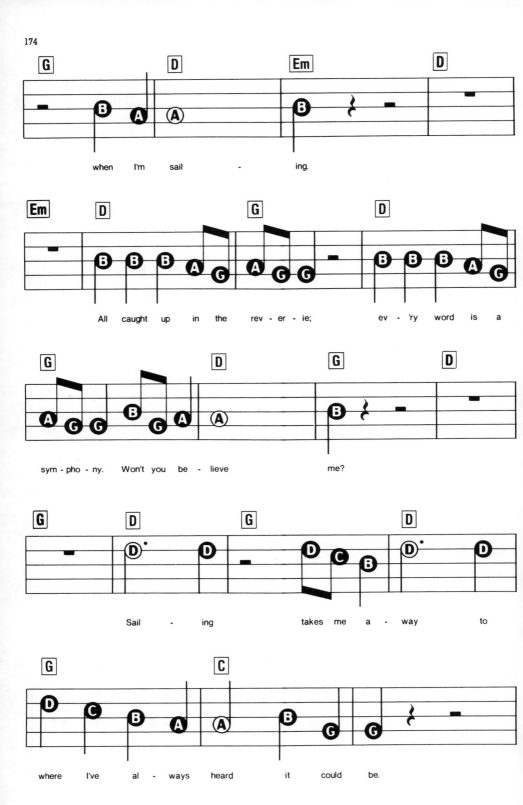

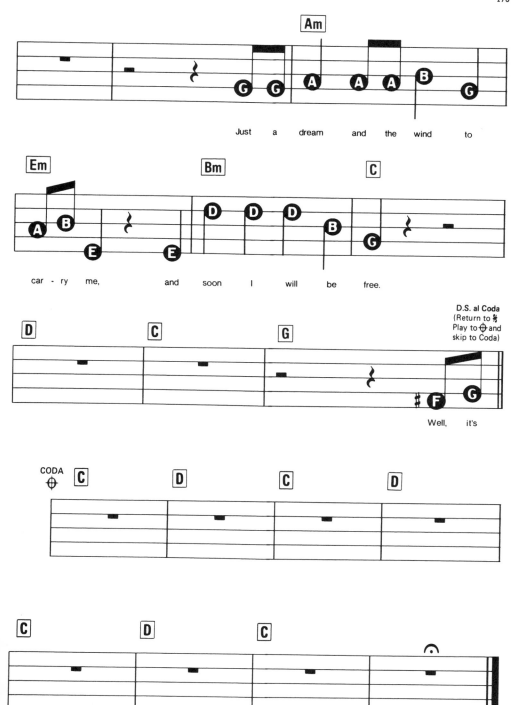

Am

Just a dream and the wind to

Em **Bm** **C**

car - ry me, and soon I will be free.

D **C** **G**

D.S. al Coda
(Return to 𝄋
Play to ⨁ and
skip to Coda)

Well, it's

CODA
⨁ **C** **D** **C** **D**

C **D** **C**

She's Always a Woman

Registration 4
Rhythm: Waltz

Words and Music by
Billy Joel

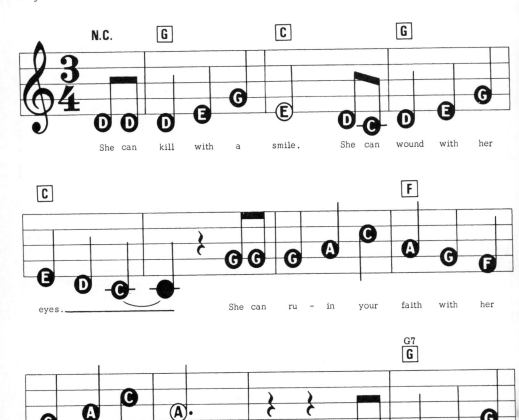

She can kill with a smile. She can wound with her eyes._____ She can ru - in your faith with her cas - u - al lies.

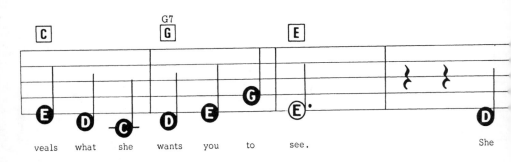

And she on - ly re - veals what she wants you to see. She

177

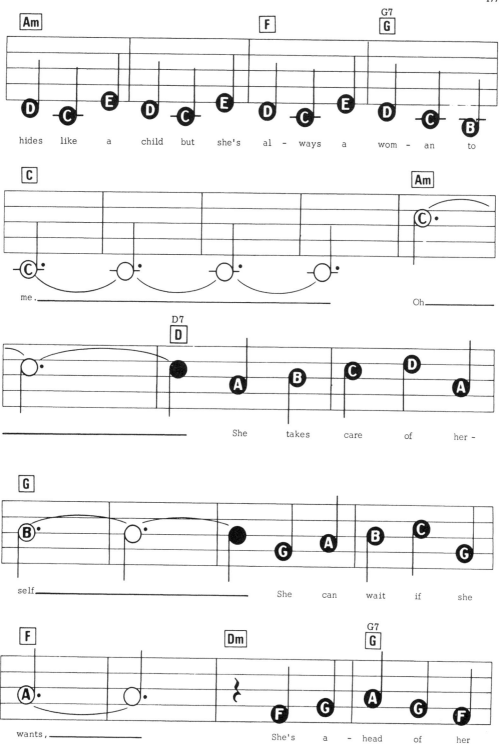

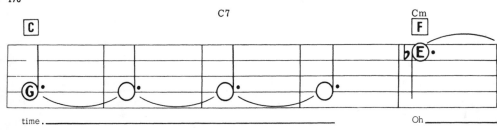

time. _____ Oh _____

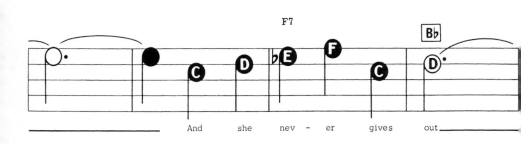

_____ And she nev - er gives out____

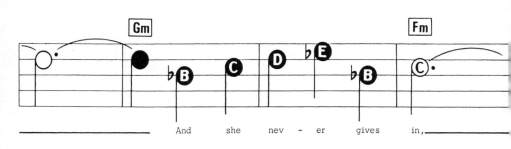

_____ And she nev - er gives in, ____

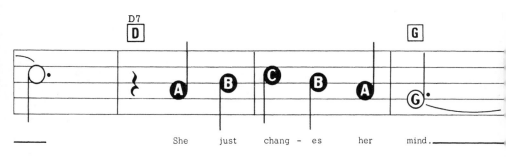

____ She just chang - es her mind. ____

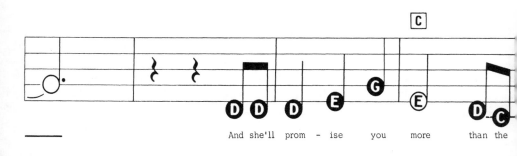

____ And she'll prom - ise you more than the

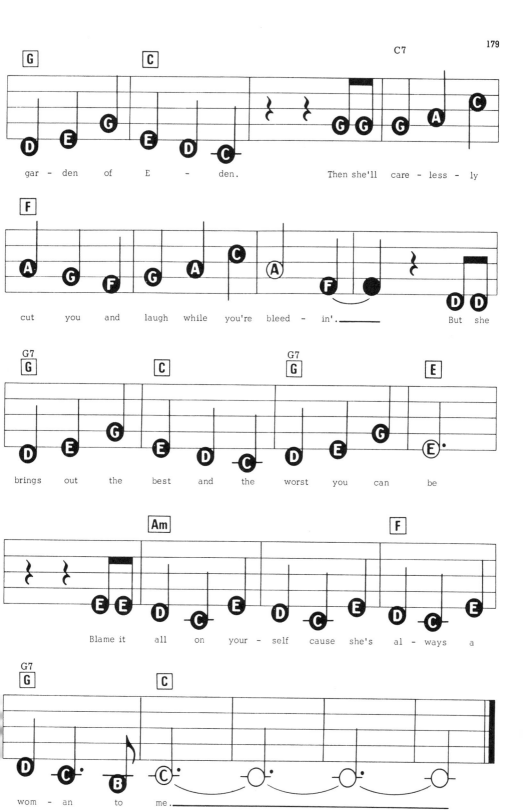

Sometimes When We Touch

Registration 8
Rhythm: Rock or Slow Rock

Words by Dan Hill
Music by Barry Mann

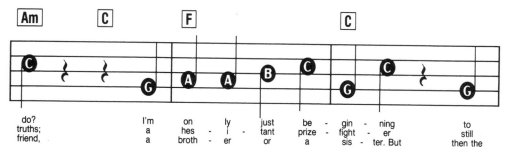

do? / truths; / friend,

I'm / a / a — on / hes / broth — ly / i — er — just / tant / or — be / prize / a — gin / fight / sis — ning / er / ter. But — to / still / then the

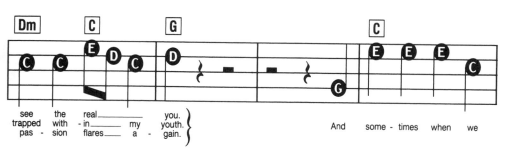

see / trapped / pas — the / with / sion — real / - in / flares — my / a — you. / youth. / gain. — And / some - times / when / we

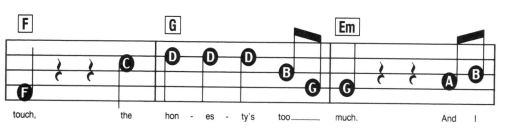

touch, — the / hon - es - ty's / too — much. — And / I

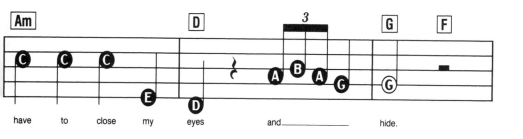

have / to / close / my / eyes — and — hide.

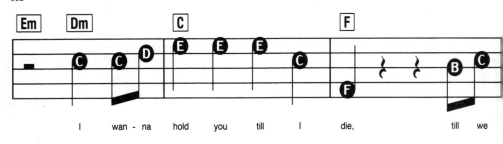

I wan - na hold you till I die, till we

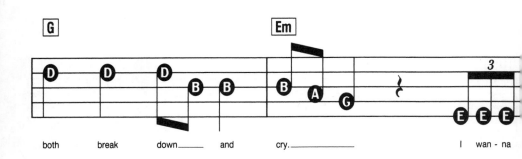

both break down___ and cry._____ I wan - na

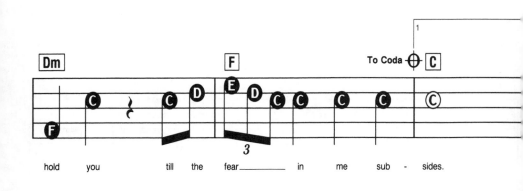

hold you till the fear____ in me sub - sides.

Ro - sides.

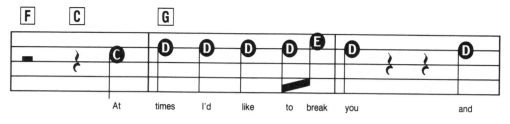

At times I'd like to break you and

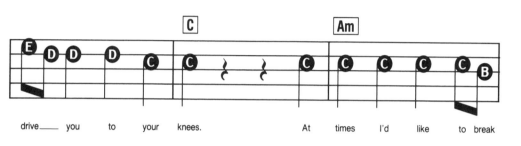

drive____ you to your knees. At times I'd like to break

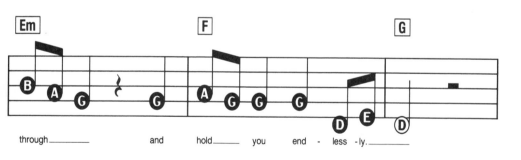

through____ and hold____ you end - less - ly.____

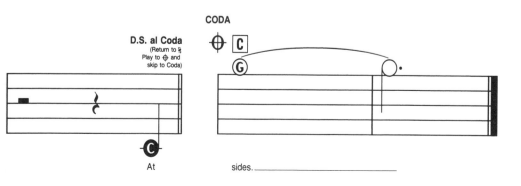

CODA

D.S. al Coda
(Return to 𝄋
Play to ⊕ and
skip to Coda)

At

sides.____

Somewhere Out There
from AN AMERICAN TAIL

Registration 3
Rhythm: Ballad or 8-Beat

Music by Barry Mann and James Horner
Lyric by Cynthia Weil

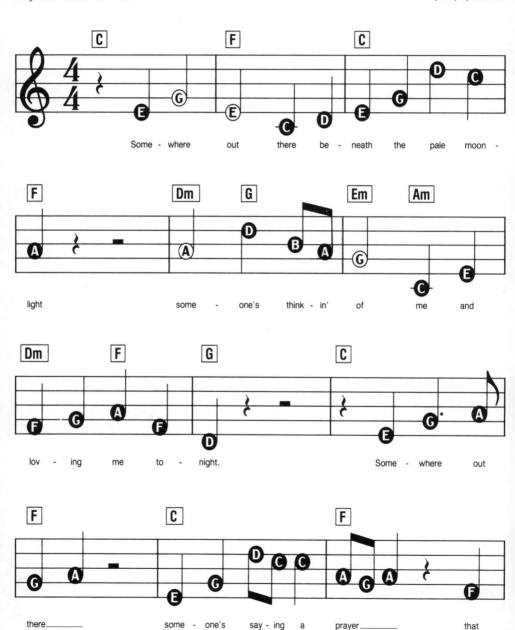

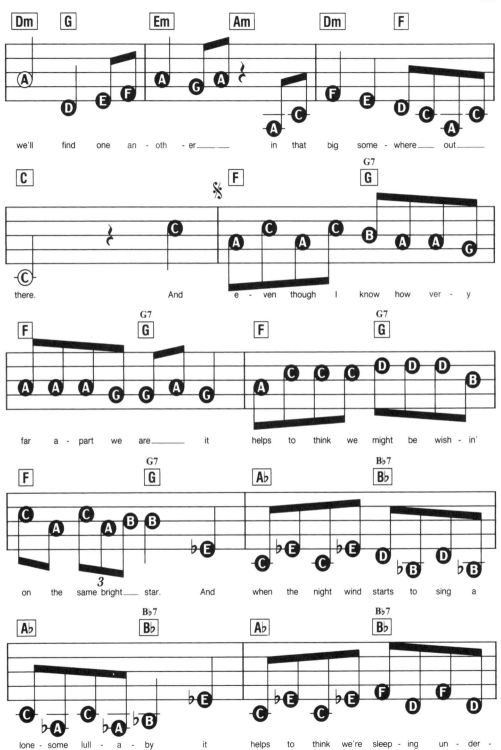

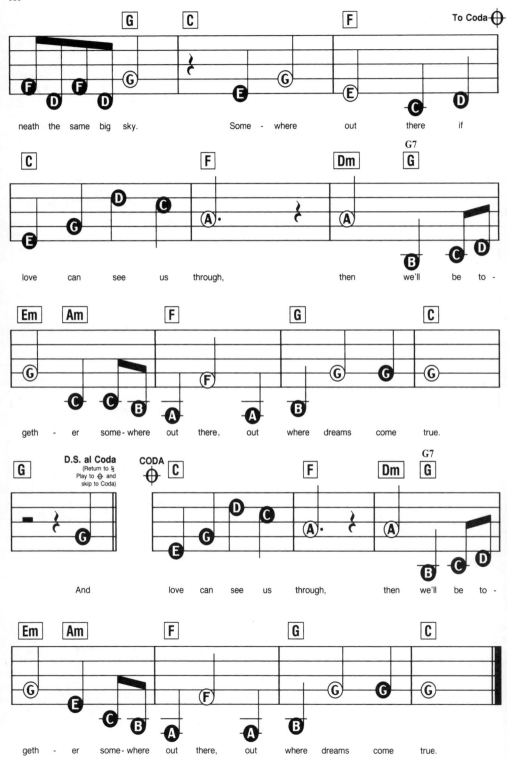

Sundown

Registration 4
Rhythm: Rock or Slow Rock

Words and Music by
Gordon Lightfoot

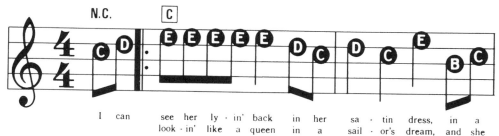

I can see her ly-in' back in her sa-tin dress, in a
look-in' like a queen in a sail-or's dream, and she

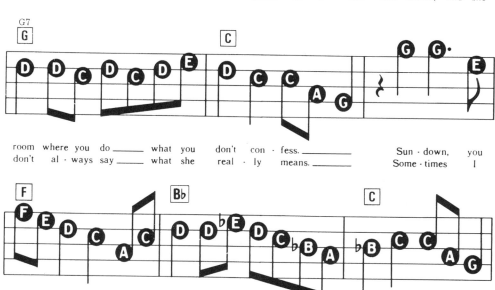

room where you do _____ what you don't con-fess. _____ Sun-down, you
don't al-ways say _____ what she real-ly means. _____ Some-times I

bet-ter take care if I find you bin creep-in' round, __ my back stairs. _____
think it's a shame when I get feel-in' bet-ter when I'm feel-in' no pain _____

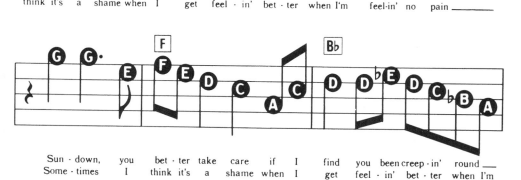

Sun-down, you bet-ter take care if I find you been creep-in' round __
Some-times I think it's a shame when I get feel-in' bet-ter when I'm

my   back   stairs   She's   been
feel-in'   no   pain.   I   can

pic - ture   ev - 'ry   move   that   a   man   could   make   get - ting
see   her   look - in'   fast   in   her   fa - ded   jeans,   she's   a

lost   in   her   lov - in'   is   your   first   mis - take.   Sun - down,   you
hard   lov - in'   wom - an,   got   me   feel - in'   mean.   Some - times   I

bet - ter   take   care,   if   I   find   you   bin   creep - in'   round _____
think   it's   a   shame   when   I   get   feel - in'   bet - ter   when   I'm

my   back   stairs. _____   Some - times   I   think   it's   a   sin   when   I
feel - in'   no   pain. _____   Sun - down,   you   bet - ter   take   care   if   I

Song Sung Blue

Registration 2
Rhythm: Fox Trot

Words and Music by
Neil Diamond

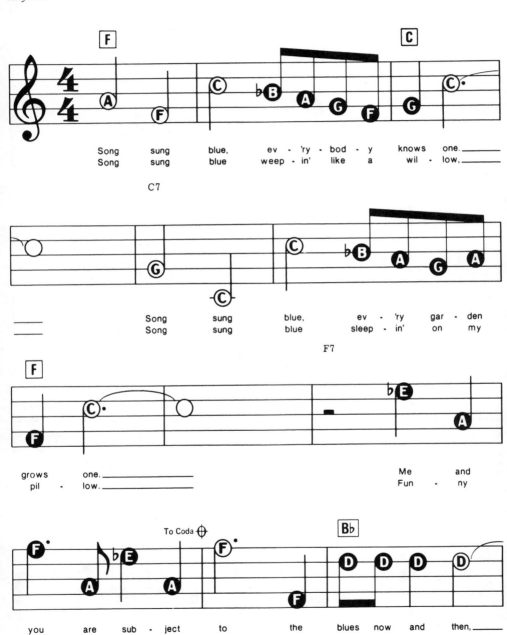

191

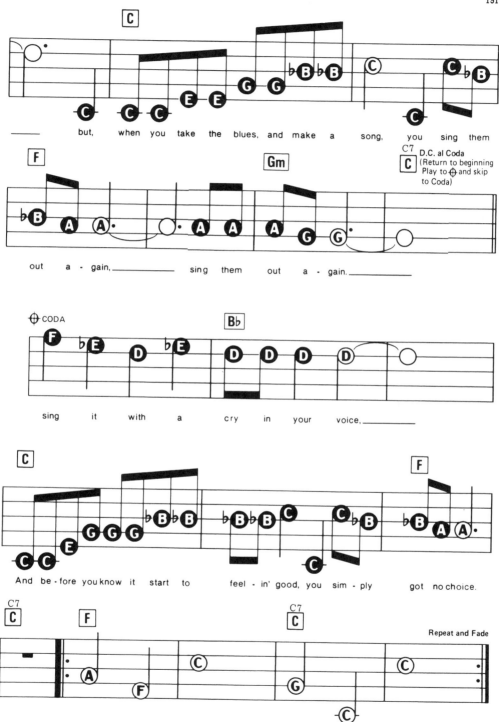

Stuck in the Middle with You

Registration 4
Rhythm: Rock

Words and Music by Gerry Rafferty
and Joe Egan

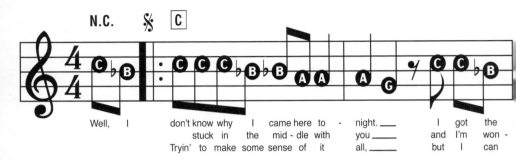

Well, I
don't know why I came here to - night. ____ I got the
stuck in the mid - dle with you ____ and I'm won -
Tryin' to make some sense of it all, ____ but I can

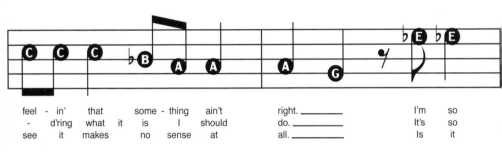

feel - in' that some - thing ain't right. _____ I'm so
- d'ring what it is I should do. _____ It's so
see it makes no sense at all. _____ Is it

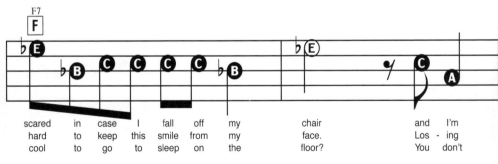

scared in case I fall off my chair and I'm
hard to keep this smile from my face. Los - ing
cool to go to sleep on the floor? You don't

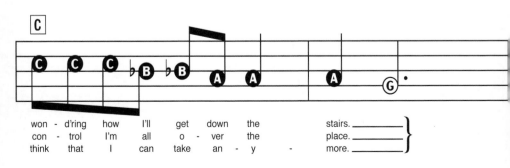

won - d'ring how I'll get down the stairs. _____
con - trol I'm all o - ver the place. _____
think that I can take an - y - more. _____

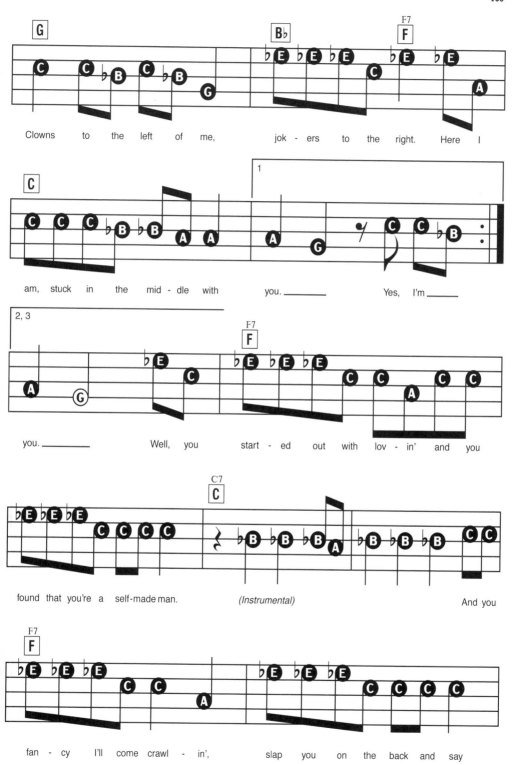

194

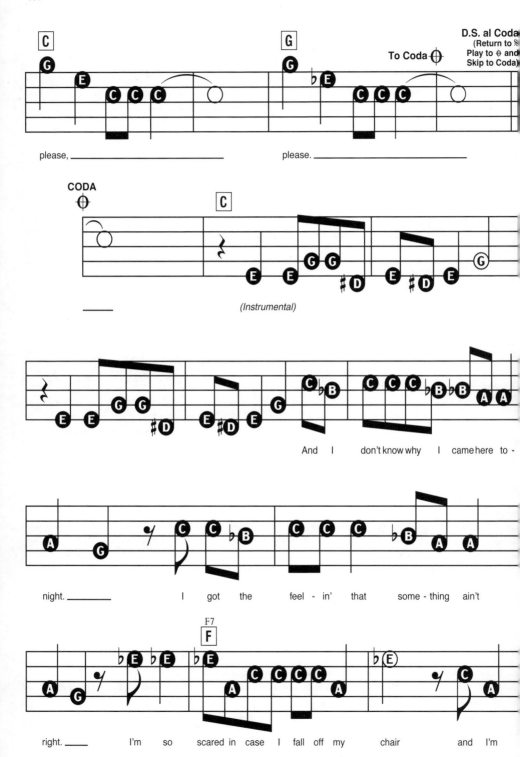

To Coda θ

please, _____

please. _____

CODA

(Instrumental)

And I don't know why I came here to -

night. _____ I got the feel - in' that some - thing ain't

right. _____ I'm so scared in case I fall off my chair and I'm

195

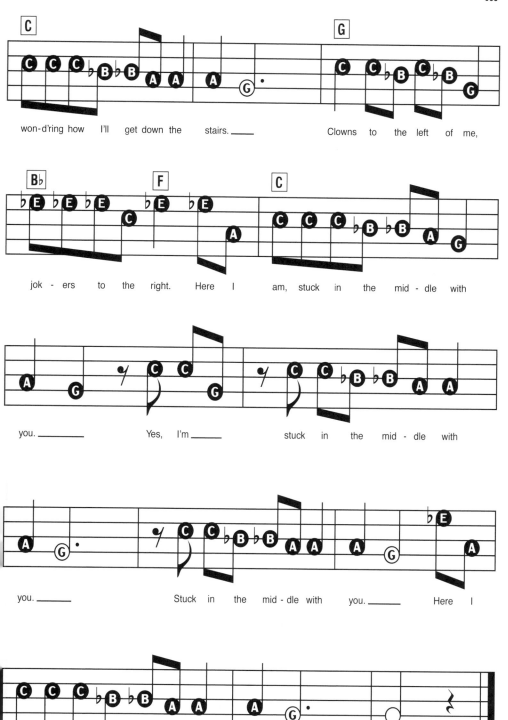

Summer Breeze

Registration 7
Rhythm: Rock or Ballad

Words and Music by James Seals
and Dash Crofts

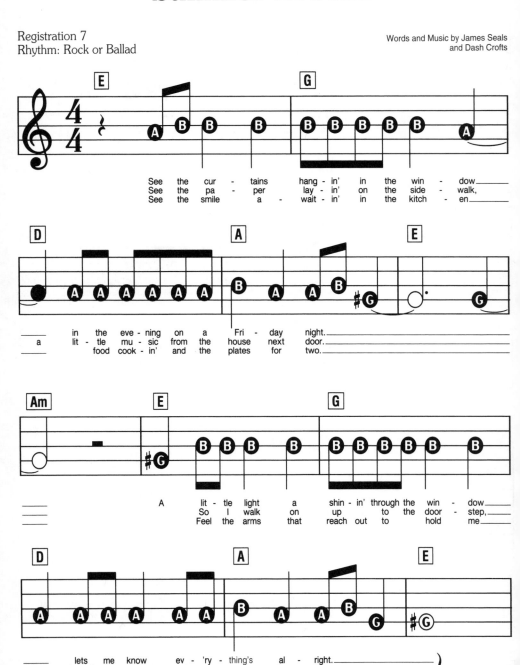

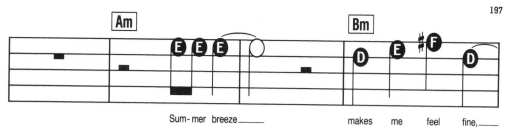

Sum- mer breeze____ makes me feel fine,____

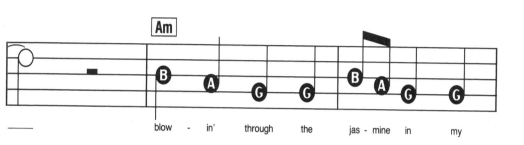

____ blow - in' through the jas - mine in my

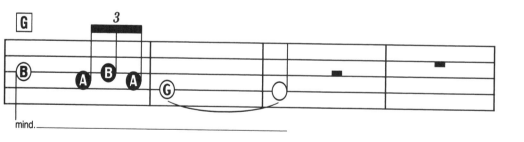

mind.____

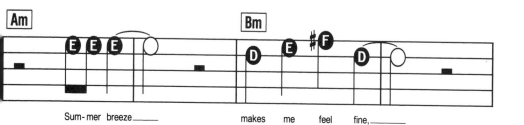

Sum- mer breeze____ makes me feel fine,____

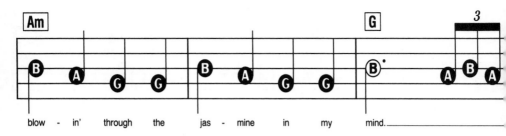

blow - in' through the jas - mine in my mind.

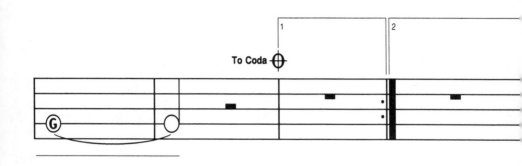

To Coda

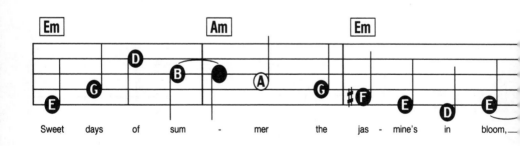

Sweet days of sum - mer the jas - mine's in bloom,

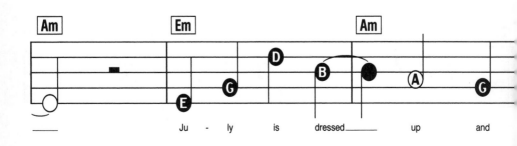

Ju - ly is dressed____ up and

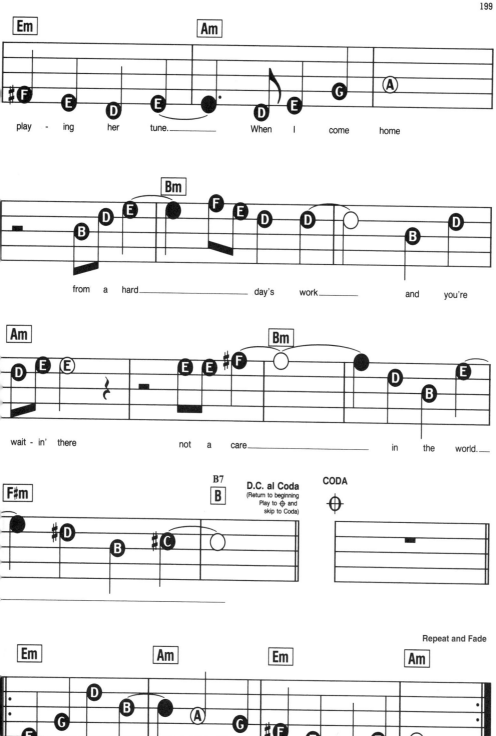

Take It to the Limit

Registration 3
Rhythm: Waltz

Words and Music by Glenn Frey,
Don Henley and Randy Meisner

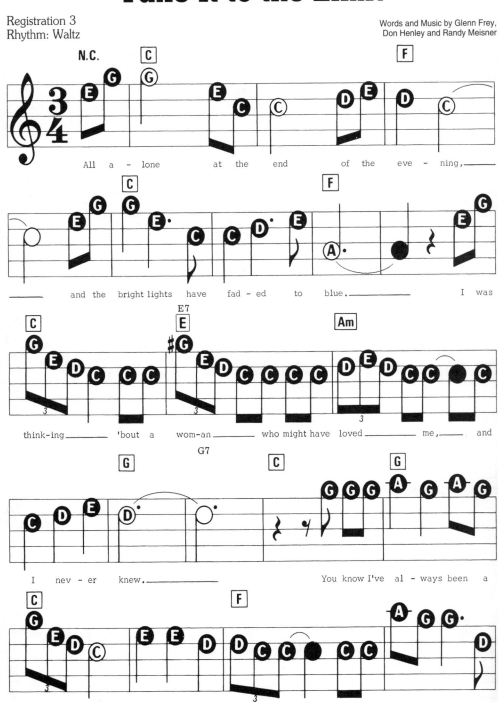

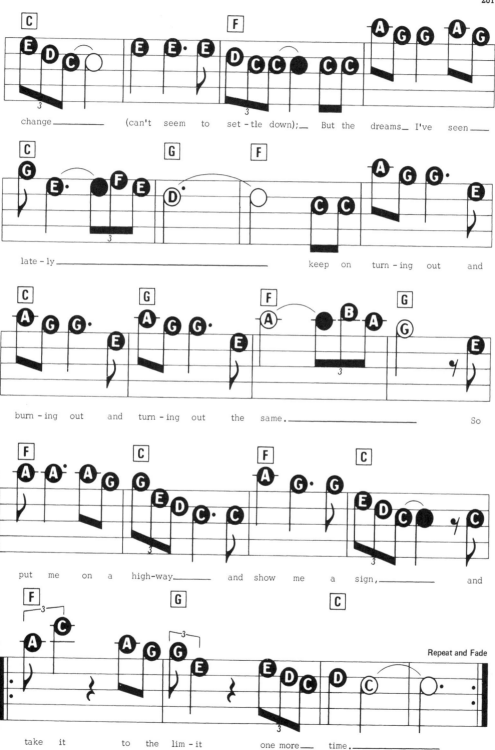

change_____ (can't seem to set-tle down);_ But the dreams_ I've seen_____

late-ly_____ keep on turn-ing out and

burn-ing out and turn-ing out the same._____ So

put me on a high-way_____ and show me a sign,_____ and

take it to the lim-it one more___ time._____

Three Times a Lady

Registration 1
Rhythm: Waltz

Words and Music by
Lionel Richie

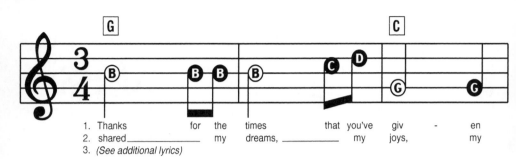

1. Thanks for the times that you've giv — en
2. shared _____ my dreams, _____ my joys, my
3. *(See additional lyrics)*

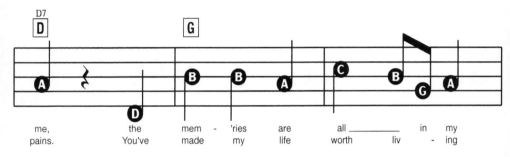

me, the mem - 'ries are all _____ in my
pains. You've made my life worth liv - ing

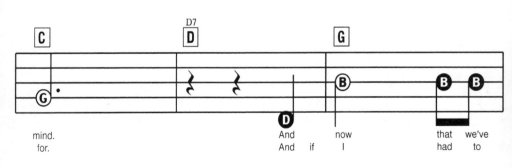

mind. And now that we've
for. And if I had to

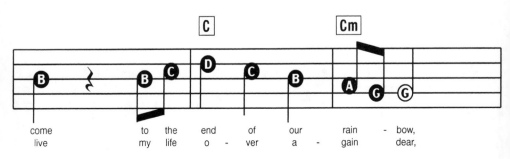

come to the end of our rain - bow,
live my life o - ver a - gain dear,

203

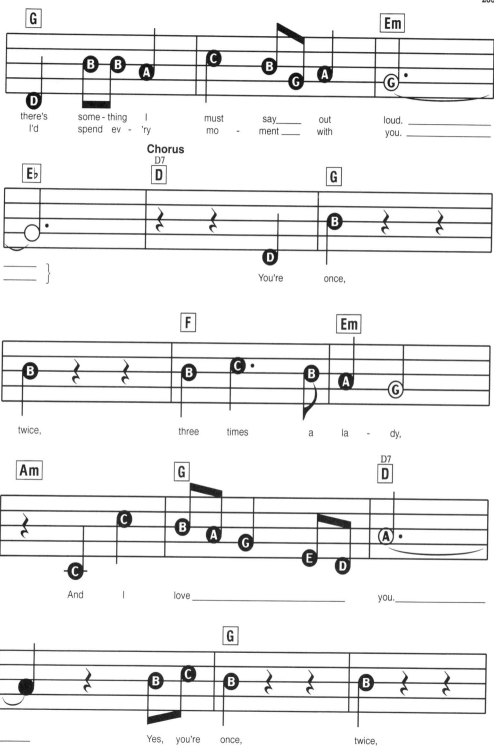

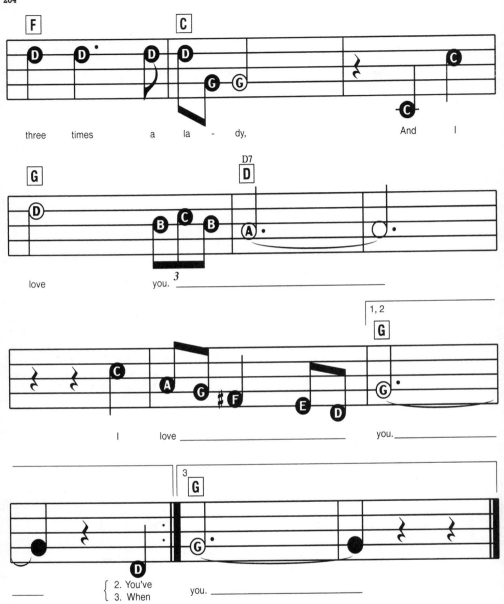

three times a la - dy, And I

love you.

I love you.

2. You've
3. When
you.

Additional Lyrics

3. When we are together the moments I cherish
   With ev'ry beat of my heart.
   To touch you, to hold you, to feel you, to need you.
   There's nothing to keep us apart.
   Chorus

The Way It Is

Registration 2
Rhythm: Ballad or Slow Rock

Words and Music by
Bruce Hornsby

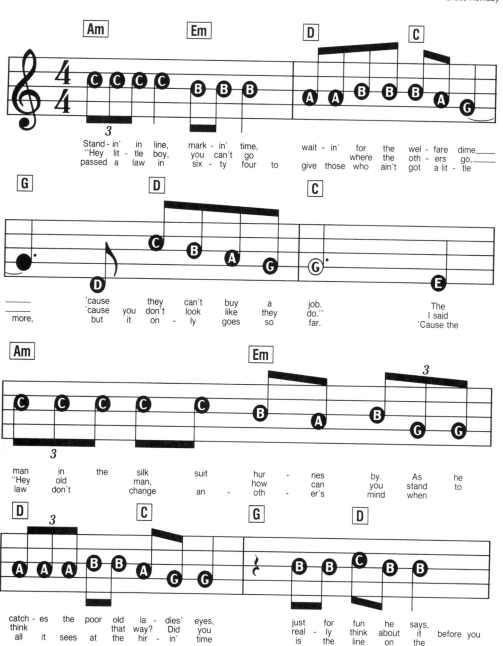

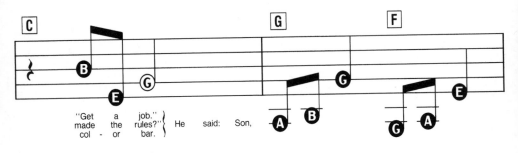

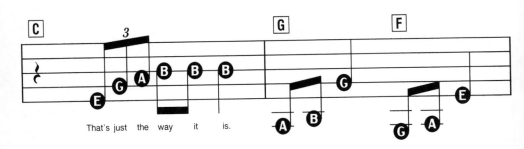

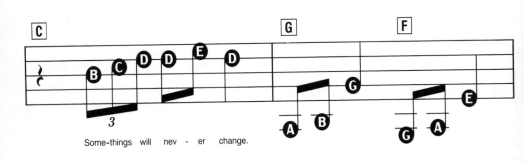

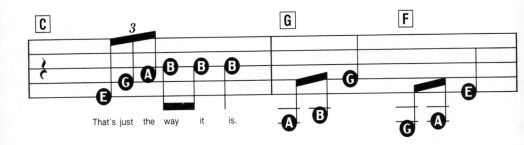

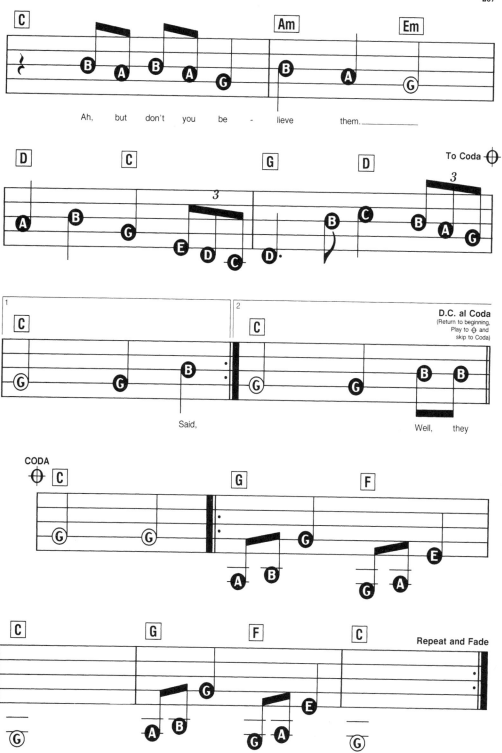

(I've Had)
The Time of My Life
from DIRTY DANCING

Registration 1
Rhythm: Rock or 16-Beat

Words and Music by Franke Previte,
John DeNicola and Donald Markowitz

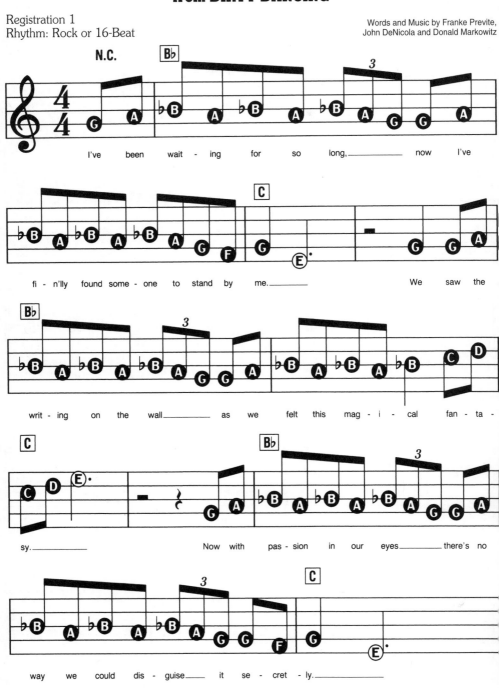

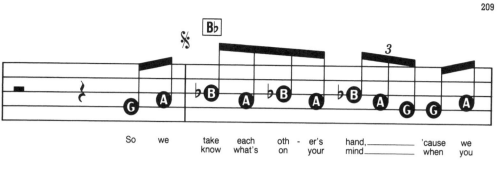

So we take each oth - er's hand,_____ 'cause we
know what's on your mind_____ when you

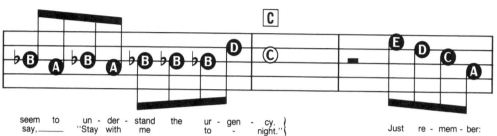

seem to un - der - stand the ur - gen - cy.
say,_____ "Stay with me to - night."

Just re - mem - ber:

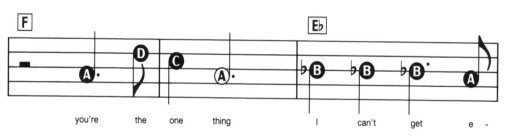

you're the one thing I can't get e -

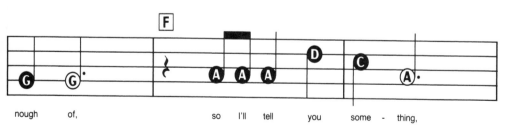

nough of, so I'll tell you some - thing,

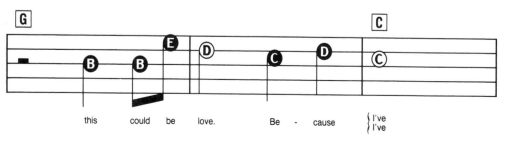

this could be love. Be - cause I've
I've

210

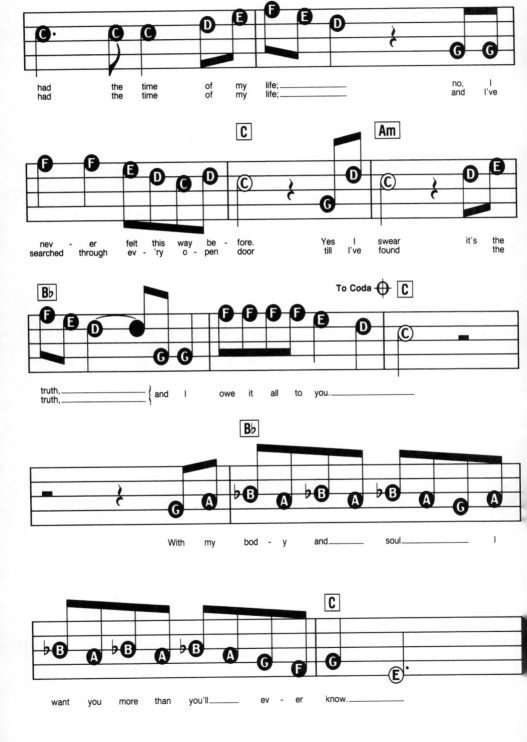

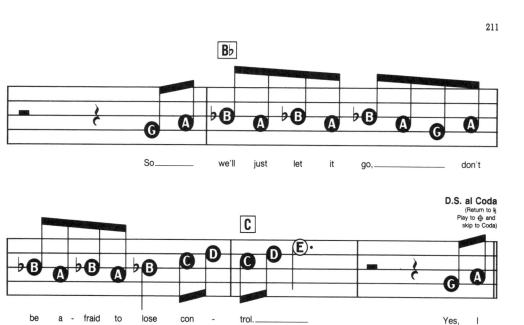

So_____ we'll just let it go,_____ don't

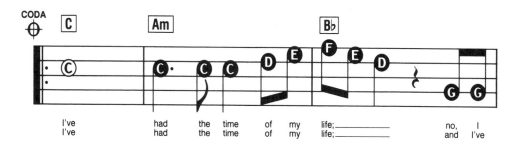

D.S. al Coda
(Return to 𝄋
Play to ⊕ and
skip to Coda)

be a - fraid to lose con - trol._____ Yes, I

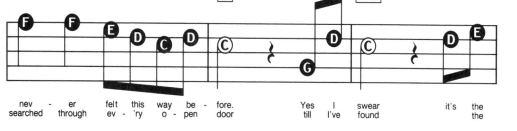

I've had the time of my life;_____ no, I
I've had the time of my life;_____ and I've

nev - er felt this way be - fore. Yes I swear it's the
searched through ev - 'ry o - pen door till I've found the

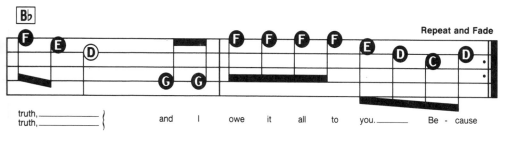

truth,_____ ⎫
truth,_____ ⎭ and I owe it all to you._____ Be - cause

Repeat and Fade

Tin Man

Registration 4
Rhythm: Rock or Slow Rock

Words and Music by
Dewey Bunnell

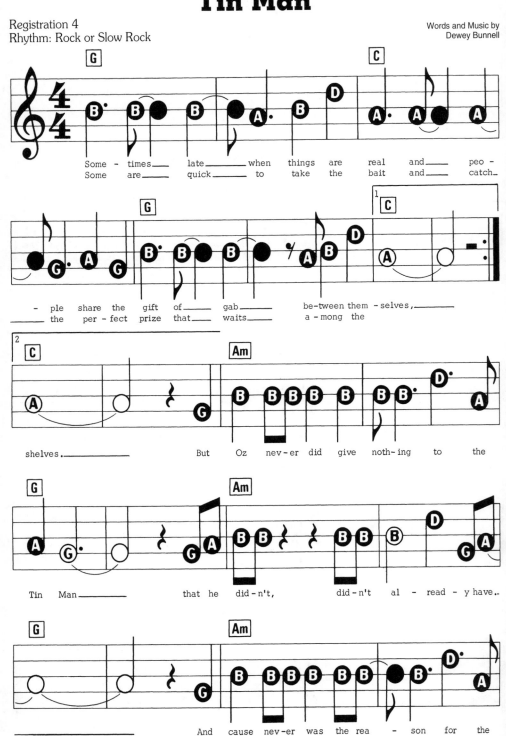

213

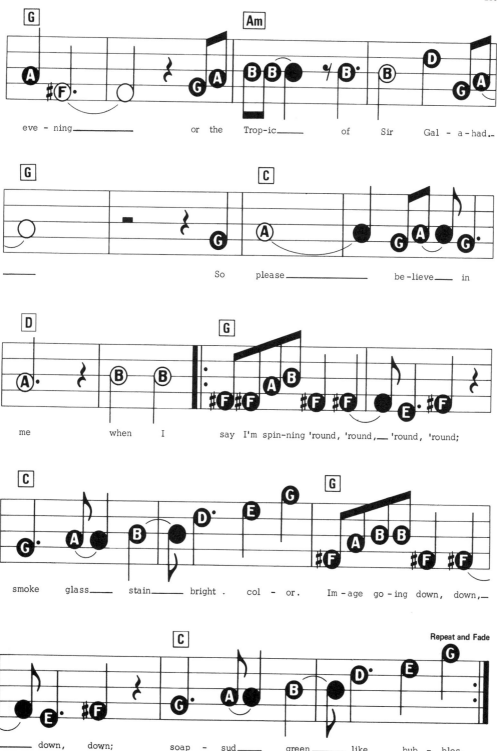

To All the Girls I've Loved Before

Registration 5
Rhythm: Rock

Words by Hal David
Music by Albert Hammond

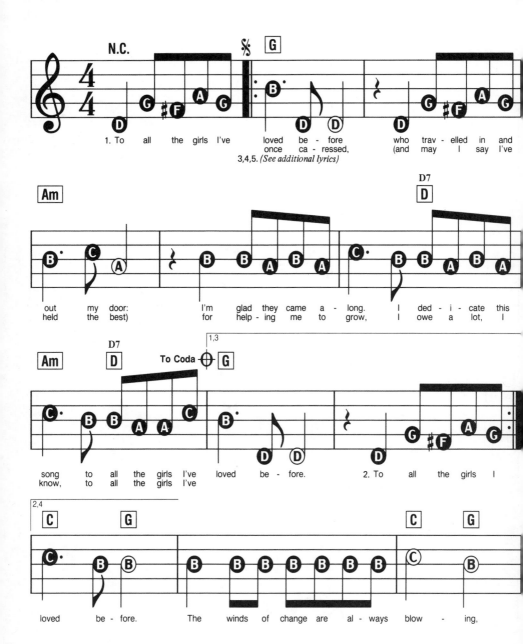

1. To all the girls I've loved be - fore who trav - elled in and
   once ca - ressed,
3,4,5. *(See additional lyrics)*

out my door: I'm glad they came a - long. I ded - i - cate this
held the best) for help - ing me to grow, I owe a lot, I

song to all the girls I've loved be - fore. 2. To all the girls I
know, to all the girls I've

loved be - fore. The winds of change are al - ways blow - ing,

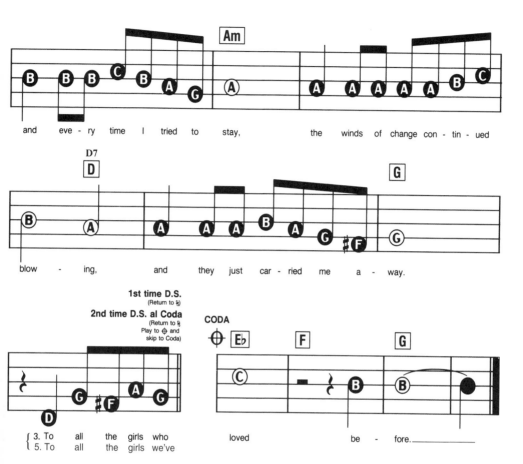

and eve - ry time I tried to stay, the winds of change con - tin - ued

blow - ing, and they just car - ried me a - way.

1st time D.S.
(Return to 𝄋)

2nd time D.S. al Coda
(Return to 𝄋)
Play to ⊕ and
skip to Coda)

CODA

{ 3. To all the girls who
{ 5. To all the girls we've
loved be - fore._____

Additional Lyrics

3. To all the girls who shared my life,
   Who now are someone else's wife;
   I'm glad they came along
   I dedicate this song
   To all the girls I've loved before.

4. To all the girls who cared for me,
   Who filled my nights with ecstasy;
   They live within my heart,
   I'll always be a part
   Of all the girls I've loved before.

5. To all the girls we've loved before,
   Who travelled in and out our door;
   We're glad they came along,
   We dedicate this song
   To all the girls we've loved before.

Vincent
(Starry Starry Night)

Registration 7
Rhythm: 8-Beat or Pops

Words and Music by
Don McLean

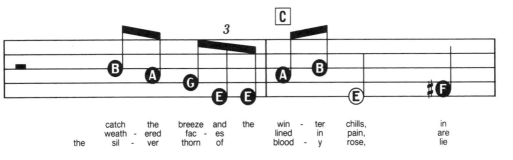

catch the breeze and the win - ter chills, in
weath - ered fac - es lined in pain, are
the sil - ver thorn of blood - y rose, lie

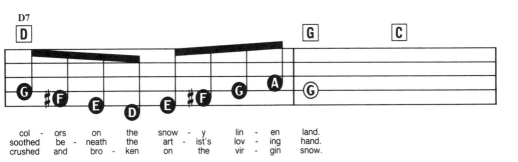

col - ors on the snow - y lin - en land.
soothed be - neath the art - ist's lov - ing hand.
crushed and bro - ken on the vir - gin snow.

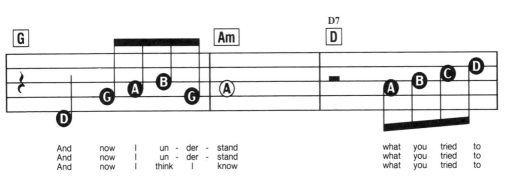

And now I un - der - stand what you tried to
And now I un - der - stand what you tried to
And now I think I know what you tried to

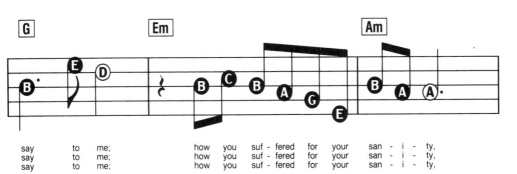

say to me; how you suf - fered for your san - i - ty,
say to me; how you suf - fered for your san - i - ty,
say to me; how you suf - fered for your san - i - ty,

218

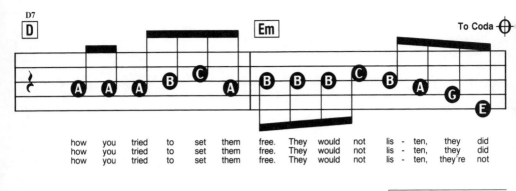

how you tried to set them free. They would not lis - ten, they did
how you tried to set them free. They would not lis - ten, they did
how you tried to set them free. They would not lis - ten, they're not

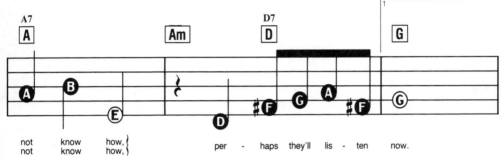

not know how,⎰
not know how,⎱ per - haps they'll lis - ten now.

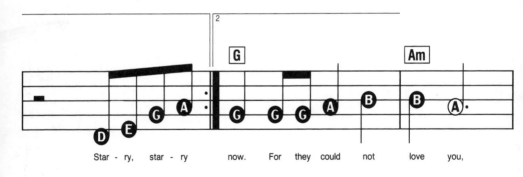

Star - ry, star - ry   now. For they could not love you,

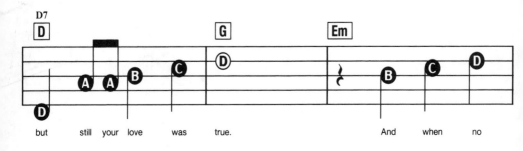

but still your love was true.   And when no

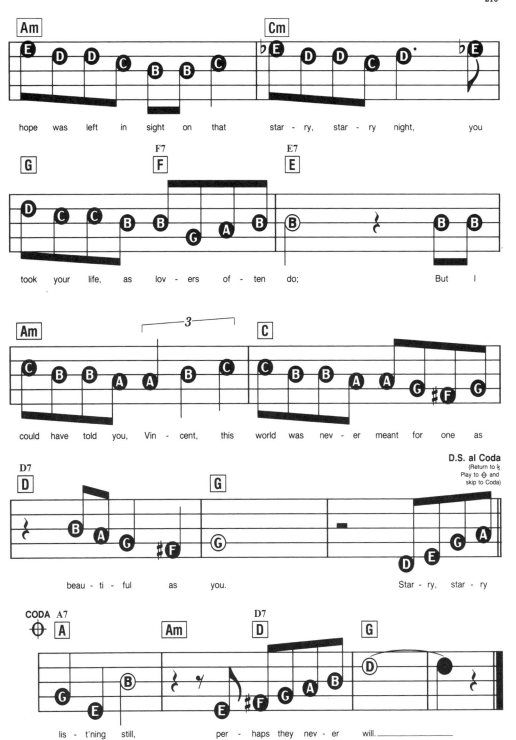

hope was left in sight on that star - ry, star - ry night, you

took your life, as lov - ers of - ten do; But I

could have told you, Vin - cent, this world was nev - er meant for one as

D.S. al Coda
(Return to 𝄋
Play to ⊕ and
skip to Coda)

beau - ti - ful as you. Star - ry, star - ry

CODA

lis - t'ning still, per - haps they nev - er will.

What a Wonderful World

Registration 2
Rhythm: Ballad

Words and Music by George David Weiss
and Bob Thiele

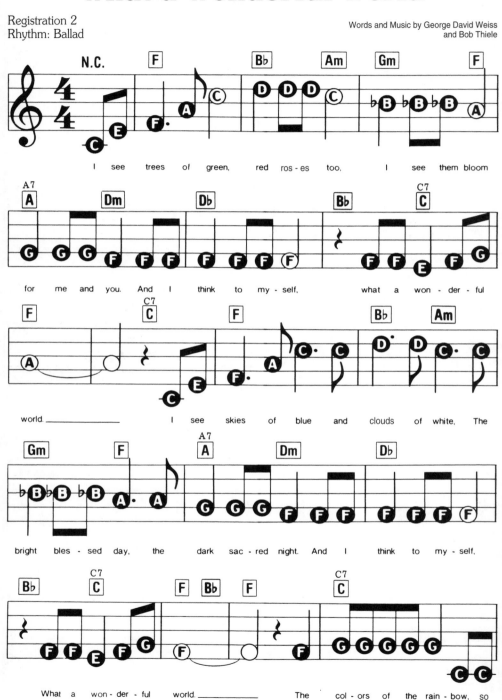

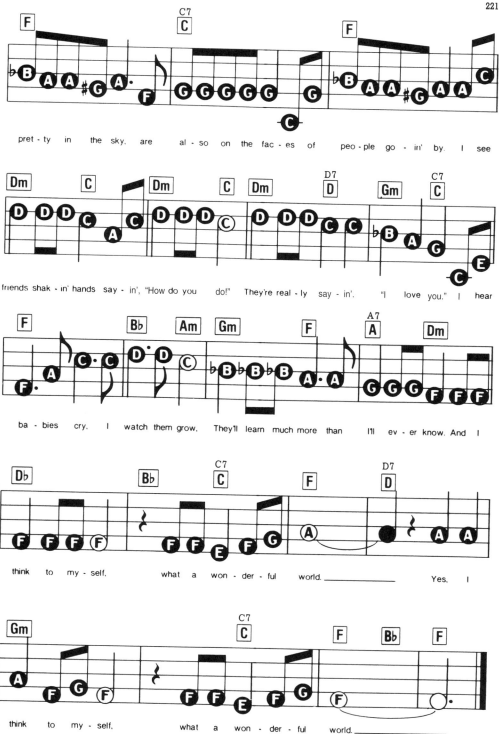

What Now My Love
(Original French Title: "Et maintenant")

Registration 2
Rhythm: Swing

Original French Lyric by Pierre Delano
Music by Francois Becaud
English Adaptation by Carl Sigman

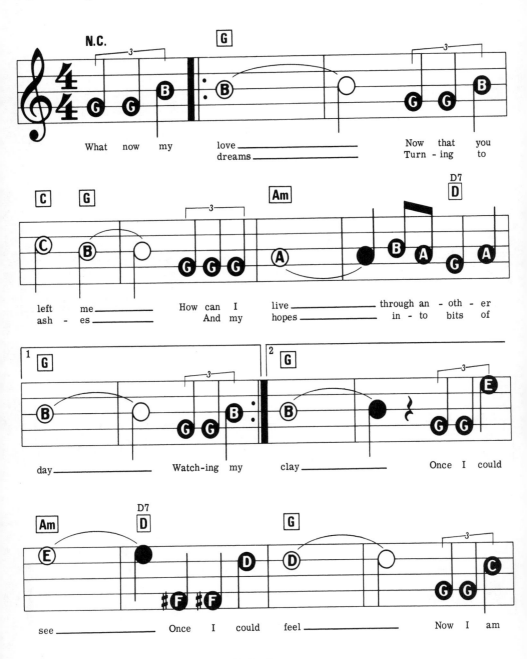

223

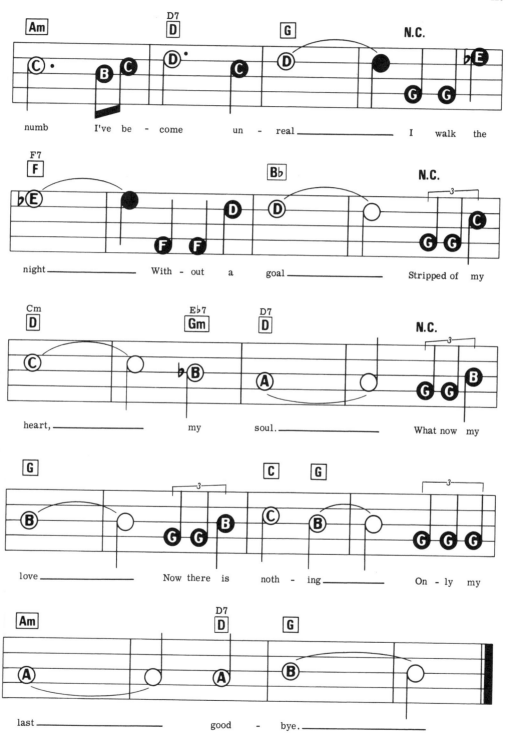

What the World Needs Now Is Love

Registration 2
Rhythm: Jazz Waltz or Waltz

Lyric by Hal David
Music by Burt Bacharach

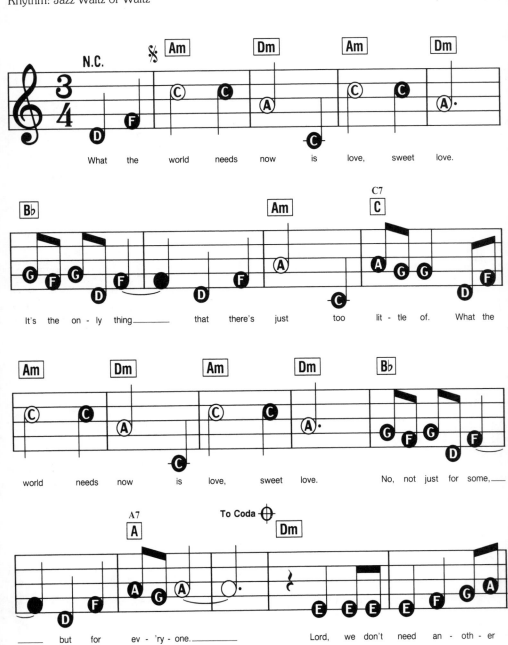

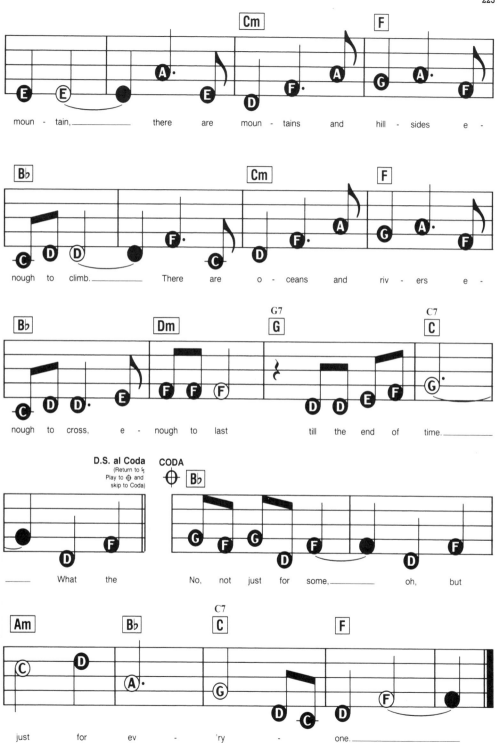

The Wind Beneath My Wings

from the Original Motion Picture BEACHES

Registration 3
Rhythm: Rock

Words and Music by Larry Henley
and Jeff Silbar

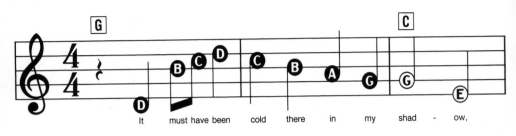

It must have been cold there in my shad - ow,

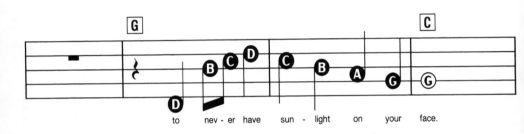

to nev - er have sun - light on your face.

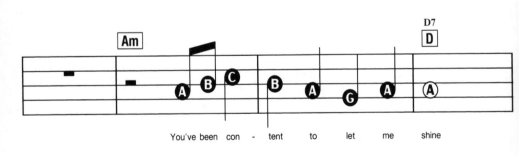

You've been con - tent to let me shine

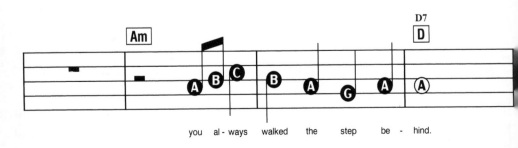

you al - ways walked the step be - hind.

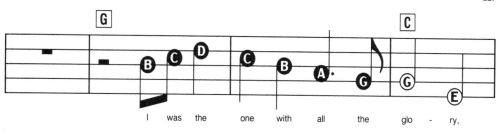

I was the one with all the glo - ry,

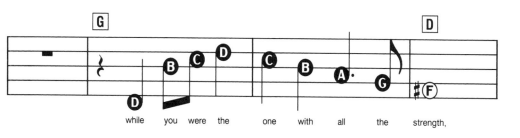

while you were the one with all the strength,

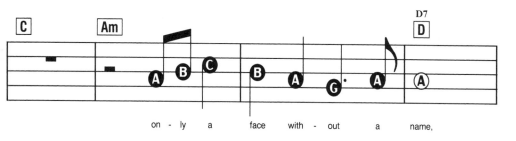

on - ly a face with - out a name,

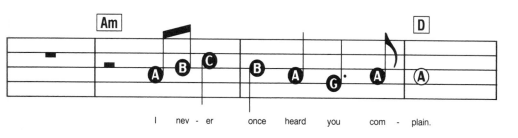

I nev - er once heard you com - plain.

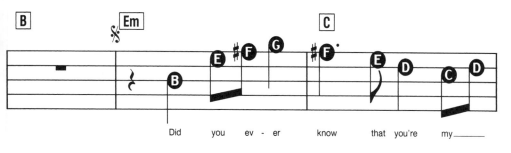

Did you ev - er know that you're my____

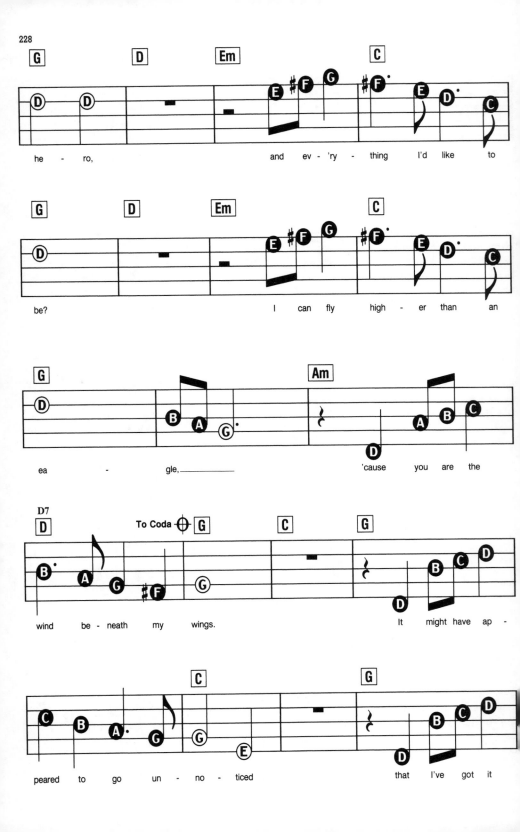

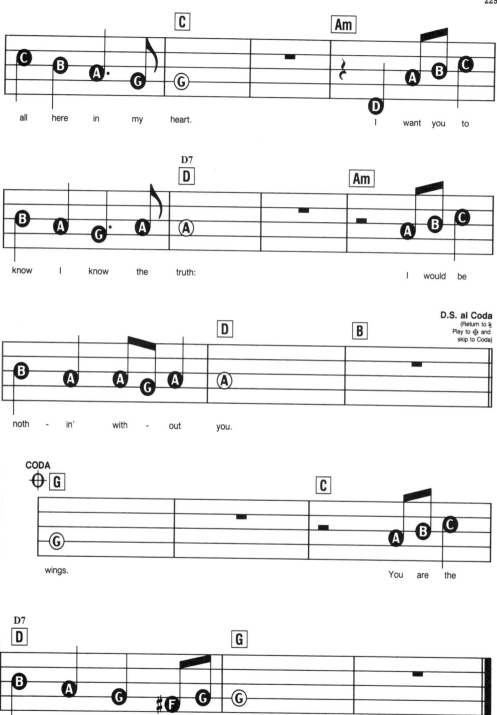

all here in my heart.   I want you to

know I know the truth: I would be

noth - in' with - out you.

wings.   You are the

wind be - neath my____ wings.

You're Beautiful

Registration 1
Rhythm: 8-Beat or Rock

Words and Music by James Blunt,
Sacha Skarbek and Amanda Ghost

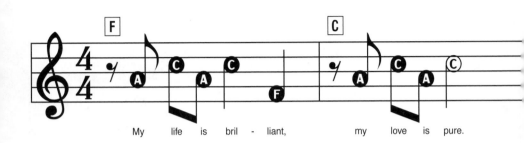

My life is bril - liant, my love is pure.

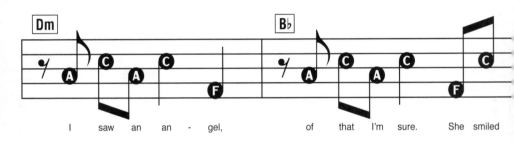

I saw an an - gel, of that I'm sure. She smiled

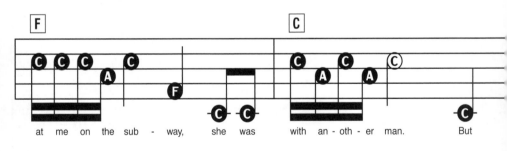

at me on the sub - way, she was with an - oth - er man. But

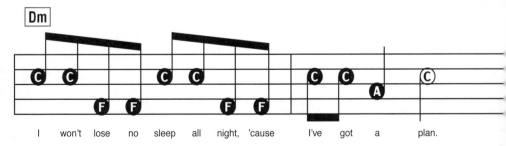

I won't lose no sleep all night, 'cause I've got a plan.

Yes, she caught my eye as I walked on by. She could see from my face that I was high.___ And I don't ___ think that I'll see her a - gain, but we shared a mo - ment that will last till the end.

D.S. al Coda
(Return to %
Play to ⊕ and
Skip to Coda)

CODA

you.

La, la, la, la.   La, la, la, la.   La, la, la, la,

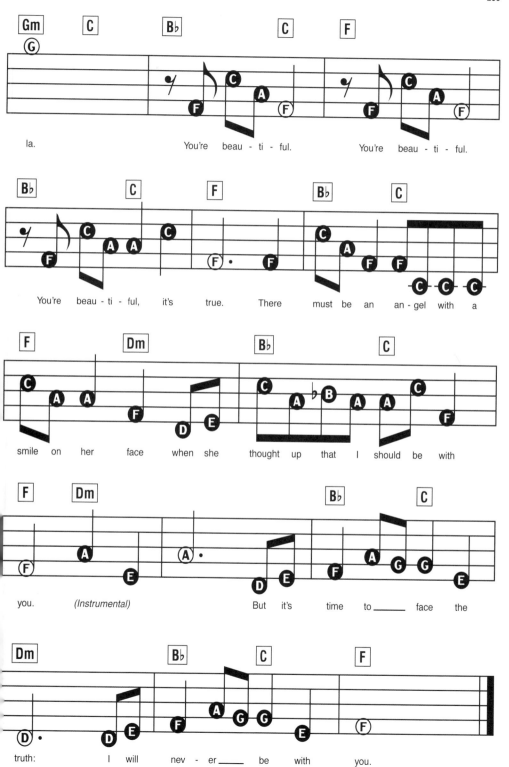

You're the Inspiration

Registration 1
Rhythm: Slow Rock

Words and Music by Peter Cetera
and David Foster

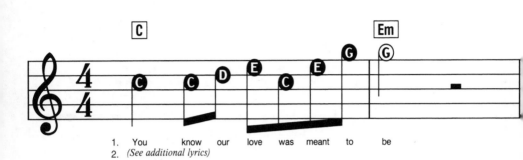

1. You know our love was meant to be
2. *(See additional lyrics)*

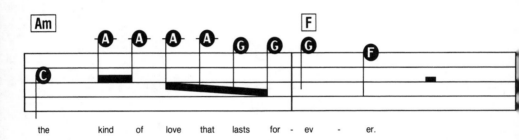

the kind of love that lasts for - ev - er.

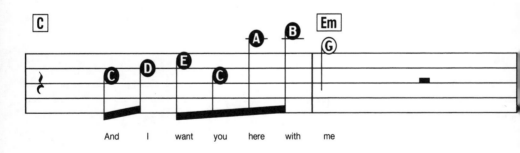

And I want you here with me

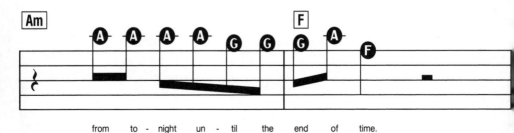

from to - night un - til the end of time.

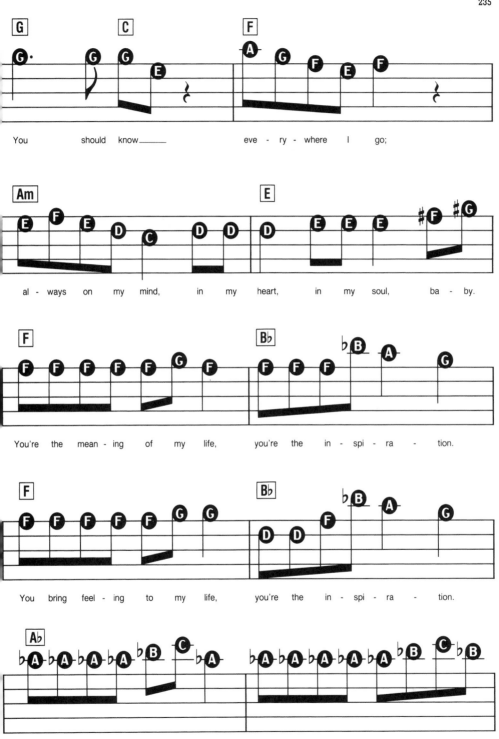

236

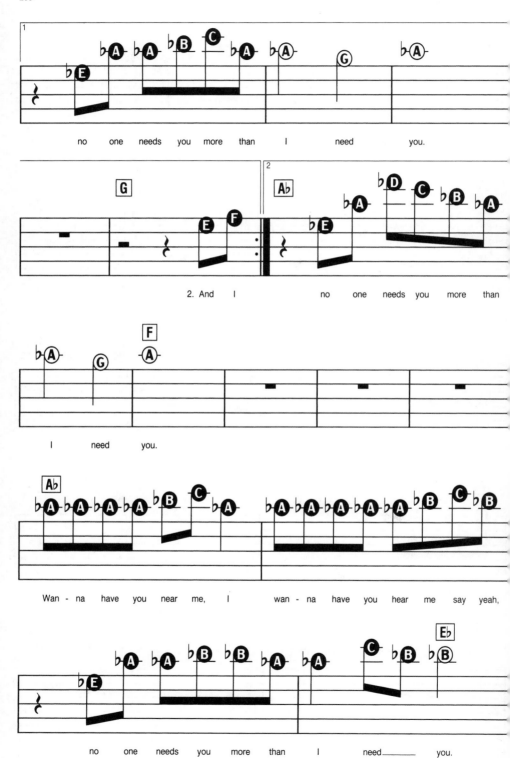

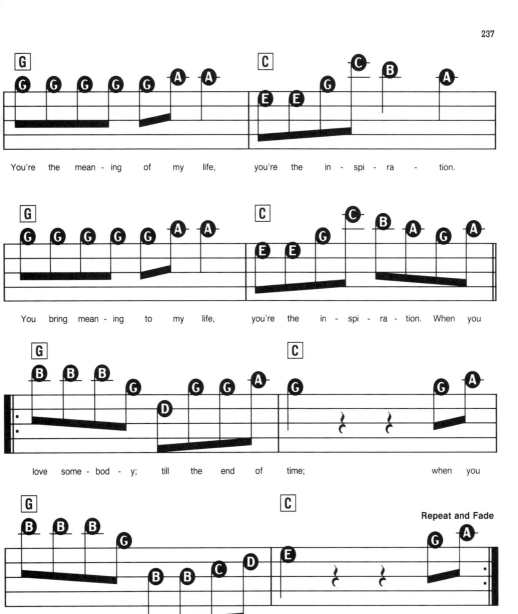

You're the mean-ing of my life, you're the in-spi-ra-tion.

You bring mean-ing to my life, you're the in-spi-ra-tion. When you

love some-bod-y; till the end of time; when you

love some-bod-y; al-ways on my mind. When you

Repeat and Fade

Additional Lyrics

2. And I know (yes, I know)
That it's plain to see
We're so in love when we're together.
Now I know (now I know)
That I need you here with me
From tonight until the end of time.
You should know everywhere I go;
Always on my mind, you're in my heart, in my soul.

Your Song

Registration 3
Rhythm: Ballad or Pops

Words and Music by Elton John
and Bernie Taupin

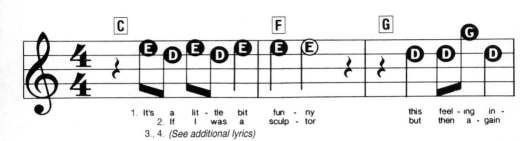

1. It's a lit - tle bit fun - ny this feel - ing in -
2. If I was a sculp - tor
3., 4. *(See additional lyrics)*

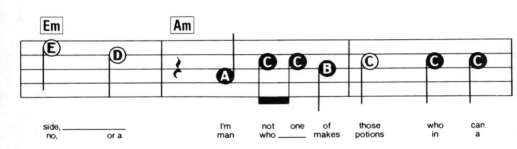

side, I'm not one of those who can
no, or a man who makes potions in a

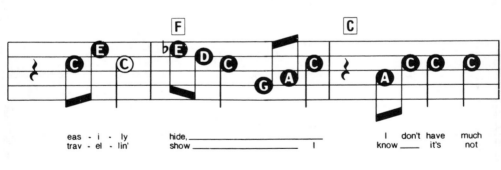

eas - i - ly hide, I don't have much
trav - el - lin' show I know it's not

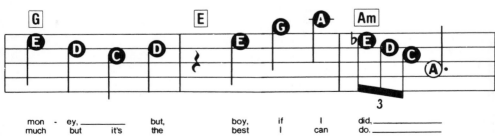

mon - ey, but, boy, if I did,
much but it's the best I can do.

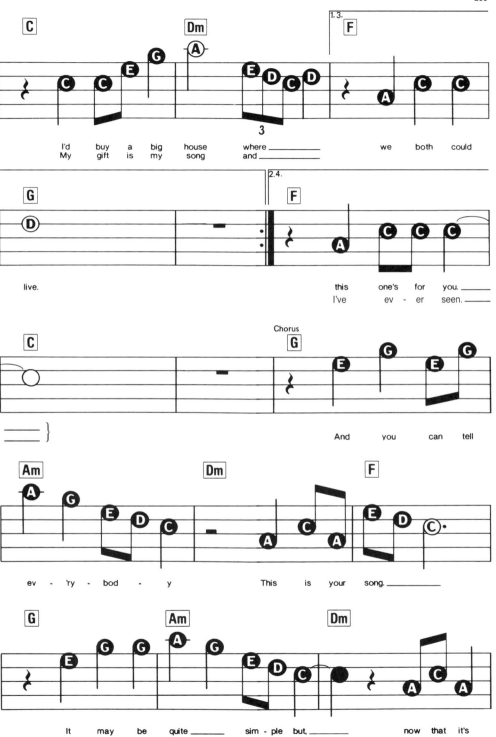

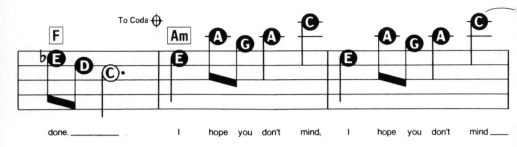

done._____   I   hope you   don't   mind,   I   hope you   don't   mind ___

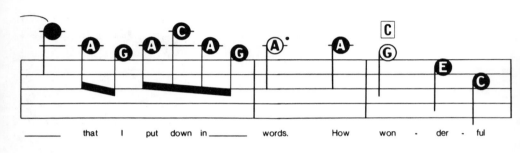

_____   that   I   put down in _____ words.   How   won - der - ful

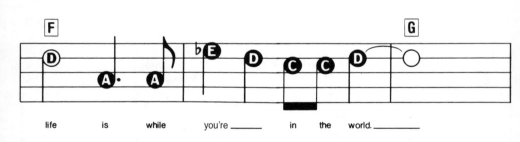

life   is   while   you're _____   in   the   world. _____

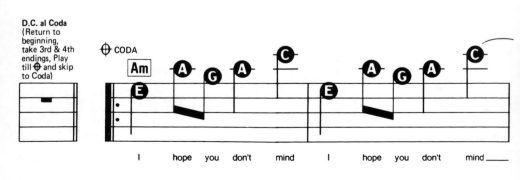

D.C. al Coda
(Return to
beginning,
take 3rd & 4th
endings, Play
till ⊕ and skip
to Coda)

⊕ CODA

I   hope you   don't   mind   I   hope you   don't   mind _____

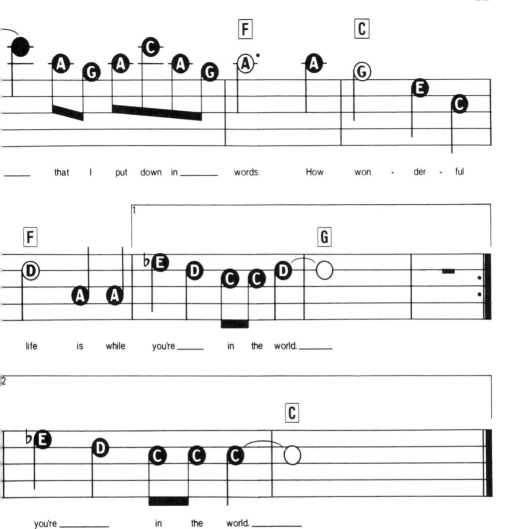

that   I   put   down   in _____ words.   How   won - der - ful

life   is   while   you're _____   in   the   world. _____

you're _____   in   the   world. _____

Additional Lyrics

3. I sat on the roof and kicked off the moss.
   well a few of the verses, well they've got me quite cross,
   But the sun's been quite kind while I wrote this song,
   It's for people like you that keep it turned on.

4. So excuse me forgetting but these things I do
   You see I've forgotten if they're green or they're blue,
   Anyway the thing is what I really mean
   Yours are the sweetest eyes I've ever seen.
   Chorus

You Are the Woman

Registration 4
Rhythm: Rock

Words and Music by
Rick Roberts

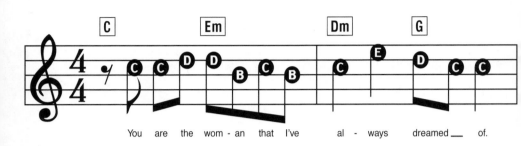

You are the wom-an that I've al-ways dreamed ___ of.

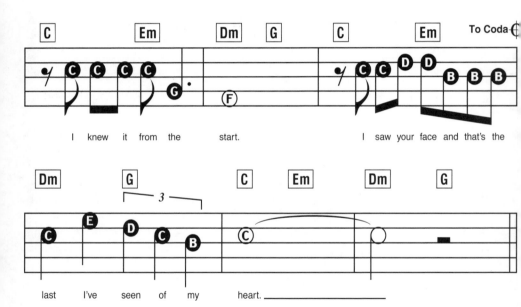

I knew it from the start.   I saw your face and that's the

last I've seen of my heart. _____

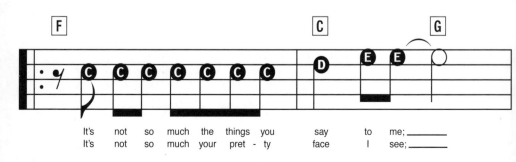

It's not so much the things you say to me; _____
It's not so much your pret - ty face I see; _____

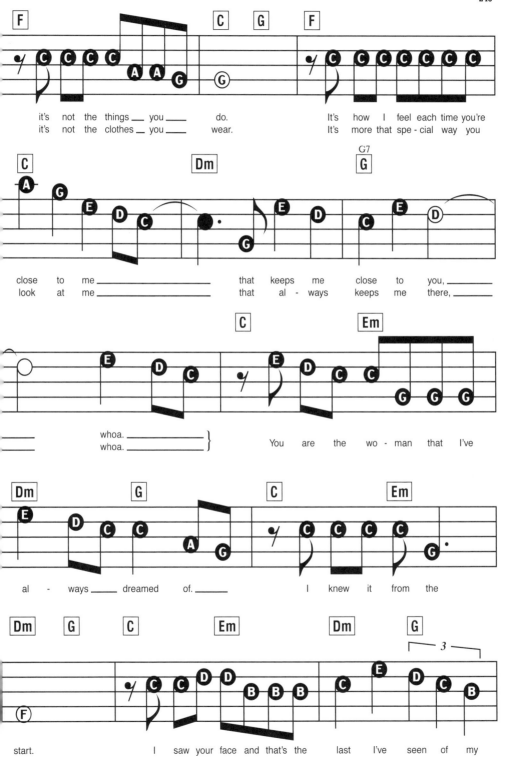

244

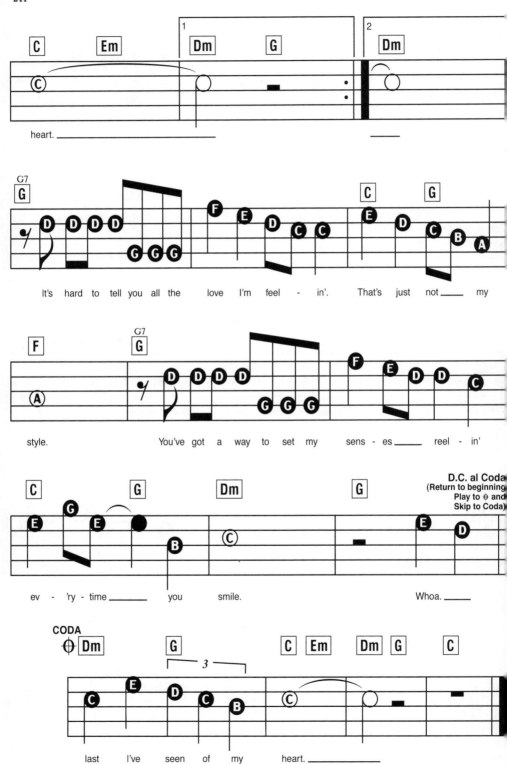

heart.

It's hard to tell you all the love I'm feel - in'. That's just not ___ my

style.

You've got a way to set my sens - es ___ reel - in'

ev - 'ry - time ___ you smile. Whoa. ___

last I've seen of my heart. ___

D.C. al Coda
(Return to beginning
Play to ⊕ and
Skip to Coda)

CODA

Registration Guide

- Match the Registration number on the song to the corresponding numbered category below. Select and activate an instrumental sound available on your instrument.

- Choose an automatic rhythm appropriate to the mood and style of the song. (Consult your Owner's Guide for proper operation of automatic rhythm features.)

- Adjust the tempo and volume controls to comfortable settings.

Registration

1	Mellow	Flutes, Clarinet, Oboe, Flugel Horn, Trombone, French Horn, Organ Flutes
2	Ensemble	Brass Section, Sax Section, Wind Ensemble, Full Organ, Theater Organ
3	Strings	Violin, Viola, Cello, Fiddle, String Ensemble, Pizzicato, Organ Strings
4	Guitars	Acoustic/Electric Guitars, Banjo, Mandolin, Dulcimer, Ukulele, Hawaiian Guitar
5	Mallets	Vibraphone, Marimba, Xylophone, Steel Drums, Bells, Celesta, Chimes
6	Liturgical	Pipe Organ, Hand Bells, Vocal Ensemble, Choir, Organ Flutes
7	Bright	Saxophones, Trumpet, Mute Trumpet, Synth Leads, Jazz/Gospel Organs
8	Piano	Piano, Electric Piano, Honky Tonk Piano, Harpsichord, Clavi
9	Novelty	Melodic Percussion, Wah Trumpet, Synth, Whistle, Kazoo, Perc. Organ
10	Bellows	Accordion, French Accordion, Mussette, Harmonica, Pump Organ, Bagpipes